Anonymous

Utrum Horum

God's ways of disposing of kingdoms

Anonymous

Utrum Horum
God's ways of disposing of kingdoms

ISBN/EAN: 9783337175016

Printed in Europe, USA, Canada, Australia, Japan

Cover: Foto ©Lupo / pixelio.de

More available books at **www.hansebooks.com**

𝔘𝔱𝔯𝔲𝔪 𝔥𝔬𝔯𝔲𝔪;

O R,

GOD's WAYS

O F

Difpofing of KINGDOMS:

A N D

Some CLERGY-MEN's Ways

O F

Difpofing of THEM.

Who is blind, but my fervant? or deaf as my meffenger that I fent?
Ifa. 42. 19.
The Prophets prophefie lies in my name, neither have I commanded them, nei-
ther fpake unto them: They prophefie unto you a falfe vifion, and divina-
tion, and a thing of nought, and the deceit of their heart, Jer. 14: 14.
O ye hypocrites, ye can difcern the face of the fky, and can ye not difcern the
figns of the times? Matth. 16. 3.

LONDON:

Printed for *Richard Baldwin,* near the *Oxford-Arms*
Inn, *Warwick-Lane.* MDCXCI.

TO THE
READER.

IT is the General *sense* of Mankind, That *Discourses upon any Particular Government, ought to be grounded upon the Laws and Constitution of that Government : And it is a Position so clear in it self, that applied to any other thing whatsoever, the contrary will appear ridiculous.* No man that were to build a Ship, would consult the Commentators upon the Book of Genesis *for the* Fabrick *and* Dimensions of Noah's Ark. Nor *is* Solomon's Temple *made the* Pattern *of our* Churches. Nor are the Laws of the Jews *observ'd by any* Christian Kingdom or State. *And yet some late Divines, in their Discourses upon our* Present Government *, and the* Settlement *of the* Nation *under* Their Majesties *, and the* Revolution *that brought it about, do not confine themselves to* our Laws, and Ancient Government, *but broach* Opinions *of their own, or other Mens* Invention *, pretended to be grounded upon* Scripture *or* Reason, *to justify what has been done ; and to persuade the People of* England, *that 'tis their duty to submit, and to plight their* Allegiance *to Their Majesties; or at least that it is lawful for them so to do. Whether the Grounds they proceed upon, are consonant to right* Reason, *the Laws of God, and of this Realm, or are not, is far from the Design of these following* Papers *to dispute.* That which is aim'd at, *being no more than to present the Reader with the Sense and Judgment of those who acted in the* Revolution ; *and who contributed their Endeavours to settle the Nation after the* Late King's *withdrawing himself ; with the Sense and Principles of some few Divines amongst us concerning these Matters.*

If the latter *run wide from the former, then it is to be feared, that those Gentlemen, who would seem to espouse the Interest of the Government , by putting* Pen *to* Paper *in Defence, or at least in*

excuse.

To the READER.

excuse of it, do it more disservice, than if they had forborn the venting their Opinions: For it cannot but weaken a well-establish'd Government, to persuade the People under it, that it stands upon another Foundation than really it does ; especially when that Foundation is not only contrary to the Sentiments of the Nation express'd, as will appear hereafter ; but is really a Fiction of speculative Heads ; and no better than the building of a Castle in the Air.

The Opposition will appear in a great measure by considering these few Particulars.

His Highness, the then Prince of Orange, *declared,* That his Expedition was intended for no other Design, but to have a Free and Lawful Parliament Assembled, for doing all things which the Two Houses should find necessary for the Peace, Honour and Safety of the Nation. To which Parliament he referred all things relating to the Succession : and promised to concur in every thing, that a Free and Lawful Parliament should determine.

They tell us of Sovereign Princes, Successes in Just Wars, *and* Appeals to God. *Whereas the Prince of* Orange *was not actually a* Sovereign Prince, *being dispossess'd of his* Principality : *Nor made war upon the Nation, or so much as upon* King James, *but came over with an Army to enforce the sitting of a* Free Parliament ; *to which* Parliament *he made his* Appeal, *and not to* God ; *though as a Pious and Christian Prince,* he relied on the blessing of God for the success of his Undertaking, in which he placed his whole, and only Confidence.

His Highness invited and required all Persons whatsoever ; All the Peers of the Realm, both Spiritual and Temporal; All Lords Lieutenants, Deputy-Lieutenant, and all Gentlemen, Citizens, and other Commons of all Ranks, to come and assist him, in order to the executing of his said Design, against all such as should endeavour to oppose him. *And accordingly great numbers actually did, and many more, nay the body of the Nation would, if there had been occasion. And when the Government was setled, Their Majesties, with the concurrence of both Houses of Parliament, Enacted, That the Oath appointed by the* Statute of

13 Car.

To the READER.

13 Car. II. *Entituled*, An Act for ordering the Forces of the several Counties of this Kingdom ; *And also so much of a Declaration prescribed in another Act made in the same year, Entituled*, An Act for the Uniformity of Publick Prayers, and Administration of the Sacraments, *&c. as is expressed in these words,* viz.

I *A. B.* declare, That it is not lawful, upon any pretence whatsoever, to take Arms against the King ; and that I do abhor that Trayterous Position, of taking Arms by his Authority against his Person, or against those that are commissioned by him : *Should not from henceforth be required or enjoined.*

But these Gentlemen tell us, That notwithstanding the unreasonable Cavils of Gainsaying Men, Passive Obedience Hickman. *always was, and they hope, always will be, the Doctrine and Practice of the Church of* England. *That Kings are the only Persons upon Earth, unto whom God has given an immediate delegation of his Authority ; whom to obey, is to obey his Ordinance ; and whom to resist, is to resist his Power.*

They tell us, That the Church of England *has been very careful to instruct her Children to obey their Princes Laws,* Sherlock. *and submit to their Power, and not to resist, tho very injuriously opprest ; and that those who renounce these Principles, renounce the Doctrine of the Church of* England. *That whatever Prince is setled in the Throne, is to be obeyed and reverenced as God's Minister, and not to be resisted. That the Church of* England *condemns all those wicked means by which Changes of Government are made.*

That Subjects have no right to make war without the leave of their Princes ; for that, as God has given to St. Asaph. *Princes the Power of the Sword, so he has forbid it to Subjects under a great penalty ; They that take the Sword, shall perish with the Sword.*

When the Lords and Commons met at Westminster, *they grounded the* Vacancy of the Throne *upon the* Late King's *having* subverted the Fundamental Laws of the Realm, and since withdrawn himself.

Whereas, according to these Gentlemens Notions, they ought
not

To the READER.

not to have gone upon a Vacancy, but have recognized the Prince of Orange's Title to the Crown, as being already chosen thereunto by God, who had given him success in a Just War against King James. Tho it would have been a hard task for them to have brought the Queen in at that Door.

And whereas the Parliament that is now in being, recognized Their Present Majesties to be Rightful and Lawful King and Queen of this Realm, according to the Laws of the same. They ought to have acknowledged him King, as being set up by God, who is not bound by Humane Laws; and the Queen, as set up by God-knows who, who is not bound by Humane Laws neither: and at the same time to have own'd, that this Providence of God in setting up the King, and this Providence of God-knows-who, in setting up the Queen, does not take away the Legal Right of the Late King; but that he having a Legal Right, may assert and vindicate it, in opposition to the Providence of God, and the Providence of God-knows-who: and that all who are not under any obligation to Their Present Majesties, may lawfully assist him in order to the recovery of this Legal Right. Tho we, who are under an obligation to Their Present Majesties, are bound to obey them, by reason of the Events of the Providence of God, and of the Providence of God-knows-who.

Other Instances of this kind might be added; and it were a very easie matter to word some parts of the then Prince's Declaration, the Votes of Parliament, the Instrument of Government, and some few Laws made since the Settlement, as they ought to, and would have been worded, if the Prince, the Two Houses, and the People of England, had proceded upon these Gentlemens Principles. But that I forbear, because it would seem scurrilous: I leave it to be the result of comparing the two Columes of these ensuing Papers.

In short, here's the Sense of the Legislative Body of the Realm, and of the People of England, set Cheek by Jowle with the Sense of a few Gentlemen of the Sacred Order; who would persuade us that our Government is drop'd out of the Skies, like the Image that fell down from Jupiter, or as the Egyptian Priests persuaded Alexander the Great, that he was the Son of their God, being convinced of it themselves, I suppose, by the Events of Providence, and his Success in a War, Just, or Unjust.

GOD's

God's Ways of Difpofing of Kingdoms:

AND

Some Clergy-mens Ways of Difpofing of Them.

THE Meafures that were taken in the late King's Reign, for the introducing of Popery and Arbitrary Power, were fo open and undifguifed, That the moft purblind amongft us, could not but fee them; and all Proteftants, that is, the whole Body of the People, were uneafie under their then prefent Circumftances, and dreadfully apprehenfive of their future. Inftead of enumerating the feveral Illegal Practices then on foot, to fubvert the Eftablifh'd Religion and Government; I fhall infert *verbatim* the Declaration of his prefent Majefty, then Prince of *Orange*, which gives a true and lively Scheme of the Condition of the People of *England*, under King *James* his Government; and grounds the Lawfulnefs and Juftice of his Arms, who had fo near a concern in the Succeffion, upon the Obligation he was under for his Princefs's, his Own, and the Nation's Intereft, to interpofe in order to their deliverance.

God's Ways of Difpofing of Kingdoms.

The Declaration of his Highnefs, William Henry, *by the Grace of God,* Prince of Orange, &c. *of the Reafons inducing him to appear in Arms in the Kingdom of* England, *for preferving of the Proteftant Religion, and for reftoring the Laws and Liberties of* England, Scotland, *and* Ireland.

1. IT is both certain and evident to all men, That the Publick Peace and Happinefs of any State or Kingdom, cannot be preferved, where

Some Clergy-mens Ways of Difpofing of Them.

A Difcourfe of Goa's Ways of Difpofing of Kingdoms, &c.

Promotion cometh neither from the *Eaft*, nor from the *Weft*, nor from the *South*.

But God is the *Judge*; He putteth down one, and fetteth up another.

TWO things the *Pfalmift* fhews in the words of this Text. *Firft,* The true Original of Power. This in *David's* time all men took where the Laws, Liberties, and Customs, established *by the lawful Authority in it*, are openly transgressed and annulled: More especially where the Alteration of *Religion* is endeavoured, and that a *Religion* which is contrary to Law, is endeavoured to be introduced: Upon which those who are most immediately concerned in it, are indispensably bound to endeavour to preserve and maintain the Established Laws, Liberties, and Customs, and above all, the *Religion* and Worship of God that is established among them ; and to take such an effectual care, that the Inhabitants of the said State or Kingdom, may neither be deprived of their *Religion*, nor of their Civil Rights: Which is so much the more necessary, because the Greatness and Security both of Kings, Royal Families, and of all such as are in Authority, as well as the Happiness of their Subjects and People, depend in a most especial manner, upon the exact Observation and Maintenance of these their Laws, Liberties, and Customs.

2. Upon these grounds it is, that we cannot any longer forbear to declare, That to our great Regret, we see that those Counsellors, who have now the chief Credit with the King, have overturned the *Religion*, Laws and Liberties of those Realms, and subjected them in all things relating to their Consciences, Liberties, and Properties, to Arbitrary Government, and that not only by secret and indirect ways, but in an open and undisguised manner.

3. Those

to be from Heaven, but from whom there, many knew not. The *Eastern* Nations, who were generally given to Astrology, took it to come from their Stars ; and especially from the Sun, which was the chief Object of their Worship. The *Psalmist* tells them, No. *Promotion cometh not* that way : Neither from the Planets rising, nor setting, nor from its exaltation in Mid-Heaven. That's the meaning of the words,

from the East, nor from the West, nor from the South. But Wisemen come out of the *East*; tho' Promotion come from the *North*: They are not Country-men.

From the *North* of the Zodiac, or from צפון the hidden part under the Horizon, they never thought it to come. And (as some think) that's the reason why that part of Heaven is not mention'd.

But the *Psalmist* might have another Reason to himself, why he did not think fit to say, it comes not from the *North*. For there (as he saith elsewhere) *on the North-side* of *Jerusalem* was *Mount Sion, the City of the great King* of Heaven and Earth. There in *David's* time was the Tabernacle, and afterwards there was the Temple, in which the Mercy-seat between the Cherubims was the place of the Symbolical Presence of God. *p.* 2, 3.

Could *David* say, *Promotion* comes not from thence ? No, he saith the contrary in the following words ; *for God is the Judge* : plainly shewing, that to him Kings owe their Authority. But

Secondly,

3. Thofe Evil Counfellors, for the advancing and colouring this with fome plaufible pretexts, did invent and fet on foot the King's *Difpenfing Power*; by Virtue of which they pretend, that according to *Law*, he can *fufpend* and *difpenfe* with the Execution of the *Laws* that have been enacted by the *Authority of the King and Parliament*, for the Security and Happinefs of the Subject, and fo have rendred thofe Laws of no effect; tho there is nothing more certain, than that *as no Laws can be made, but by the joynt concurrence of King and Parliament, fo likewife Laws fo enacted*, which fecure the Publick Peace, and Safety of the Nation, and the Lives and Liberties of every Subject in it, *cannot be Repealed or Sufpended, but by the fame Authority.*

4. For tho the King may pardon the Punifhment that a Tranfgreffor has incurred, and to which he is condemned, as in the Cafes of *Treafon* or *Felony*; yet it cannot be with any colour of Reafon inferred from thence, That the King can entirely fufpend the Execution of thofe Laws relating to *Treafon* or *Felony*; unlefs it is pretended, that he is clothed with a Defpotick and Arbitrary Power; and that the Lives, Liberties, Honours, and Eftates of the Subjects, depend wholly on his good Will and Pleafure, and are intirely fubject to him; which muft infallibly follow, on the King's having a power to fufpend the Execution of the *Laws*, and to difpence with them.

5. Thofe

Secondly, It is to him as *Judge*. He gives it Judicially. And fo to him they are to account for it. *p.* 4.

'Tis the Prerogative of God, by which He acts, both in the difpofing, and alfo in the transferring of Kingdoms.

The work God in bringing His Majefty into this Kingdom, was truly God's making ufe of the latter branch of his Prerogative, *in putting down one, and fetting up another.* p. 5.

The Powers that be, are of God: That is, the feveral Kingdoms and States, even all that are in the World, all have their Authority from God.

I. This at firft was from God, we are fure, becaufe it was from the beginning of Mankind. The firft Men that were born into the World, were all of *Adam*'s Family. *p.* 7.

Noah was the Father of all them that liv'd after the Flood.

When the Fathers or Heads of fome of thofe Nations made Conquefts upon one another, as *Nimrod* did on the Nations about him, who was therefore call'd *a mighty hunter before the Lord*; or when they were otherwife incorporated together; thefe made the ancient great Monarchies, whereof the *Affyrian* and *Egyptian* are famous in Ancient Hiftory.

Other of thofe Nations, or rather great Families, continu'd in their ancient way of Patriarchal Government. Particularly in that Line out of which God chofe his peculiar People; *Abraham* was *a mighty Prince* in his days: But all his Subjects were of his Family, out of which proceeded *many Nations.* From his Son *Ifaac* ther'

5. Those Evil Counsellors, in order to the giving some Credit to *this strange and execrable Maxim*, have so conducted the Matter, that they have obtained a Sentence from the Judges, declaring, That this *Dispensing Power* is a Right belonging to the *Crown*; as if it were in the power of the Twelve Judges to offer up the Laws, Rights, and Liberties of the whole Nation, to the King, to be disposed of by him Arbitrarily and at his Pleasure, and expresly contrary to Laws enacted for the Security of the Subjects. In order to the obtaining this Judgment, those Evil Counsellors did before-hand examine secretly the Opinion of the Judges, and procured such of them as could not in Conscience concur in so pernicious a Sentence, to be turned out, and others to be substituted in their rooms, till by the Changes which were made in the Courts of Judicature, they at last obtained that Judgment. And they have raised some to those Trusts, who make open profession of the Popish Religion, tho those are by Law rendred incapable of all such Employments.

6. It is also manifest and notorious, That as his Majesty was upon his coming to the Crown, received and acknowledged by all the Subjects of *England, Scotland*, and *Ireland*, as their *King*, without the least Opposition, tho he made then open Profession of the *Popish Religion*; so he did then promise, and solemnly swear at his Coronation, That he would maintain his Subjects

there came *two Nations of People*; one of them by *Esau*, Father of *Edom*, the other by *Jacob*, the Father of *Israel*; who for their times also govern'd those Families or Nations.

When *Jacob* and all his Family went down into *Egypt*, there ended their Patriarchal Government. After which, being Subjects to the King of that Country, they were brought into a long and sore Bondage, which *made their Lives bitter to them* for many Generations.

2. From this God deliver'd them by the hand of *Moses*. And to shew them how they ought to value this mercy, from thence he entitled himself to be their King, and dated the beginning of his Reign.

3. This *Theocracy*, as we call it, continu'd from their coming up out of *Egypt*, till such time as God, at his Peoples desire, gave them *a King to judge them like all the Nations. p. 8,9.*

God was pleas'd so far to grant his Peoples Request, that they should be an Hereditary Kingdom: But for the first King of the reigning Line, God would have the chusing of him himself. And accordingly, first he chose *Saul*. *I thought the People had chosen him by lot at Mispah.*

Then God made choice of *David*, a man after his own heart. *I thought the People had chosen David too.*

There was no other standing Government in that Nation, which God chose to be his peculiar People, but what was administred by single Persons. And those Persons Title to the Government was either Patriarchal jects in the free Enjoyment of their Laws and Liberties; and in particular, That he would maintain the *Church of England as it was Establish-ed by Law*: It is likewise certain, That there have been at divers and sundry times, several Laws enacted for the Preservation of those Rights and Liberties, and of the Protestant Religion; and among other Securities, it has been enacted, That all Persons whatsoever, that are advanced to any Ecclesiastical Dignity, or to bear Office in either University, as likewise all other that should be put in any Employment, Civil or Military, should declare that they were not Papists, but were of the Protestant Religion, and that by their taking of the Oaths of *Allegiance* and *Supremacy*, and the *Test*, yet these Evil Counsellors have in effect annulled and abolished all those Laws, both with relation to Ecclesiastical and Civil Employments.

7. In order to Ecclesiastical Dignities and Offices, they have not only, without any colour of Law, but against most express Laws to the contrary, set up a Commission of a certain number of persons, to whom they have committed the Cognizance and Direction of all Ecclesiastical matters; in the which Commission there has been, and still is one of his Majesties Ministers of State, who makes now publick profession of the Popish Religion, and who at the time of his first professing it, declared, That for a great while before, he had believed that to be the only true Religion. By all this,

triarchal, or by Divine nomination: Both which ways of coming into Power were so wholly of God, that the People had nothing to do, but to accept the Choice of God, and to submit to it.

II. In other Nations indeed, that did not keep up the Patriarchal Right, there the Peoples Consent was required, except in the Case of Conquest. *p.* 10, 11.

And this Consent being merely an humane Act, it may seem that the Authority it gives, is not, as we are here taught, from God only.

But we are to consider by what Motives it is, that the People are generally led, to chuse any one to rule over them. All their Motives may be reduc'd to these two; either Merit, or Favour. If there be any other, they are but Compositions of these.

I. The first Choice of Kings I conceive to have been made on account of Merit, the People being led to it by a sense of the Benefits they had receiv'd. I judge so from that which having been already shewn, I take now for granted, that the Earth was peopled at first by great Families. Now when those, by oppression of powerful Neighbours, or by Civil Discord among themselves, came to be in great distress, such as made them see the necessity of being united in greater Bodies for their own preservation; those Heroic Men, that shew'd them the way of it, and that brought them under Government and Laws, these were called the FOUNDERS of the Nations. Such was *Moses* among the

People

this, the deplorable State to which the Proteftant Religion is reduced, is apparent, fince the Affairs of the Church of *England* are now put into the hands of perfons who have accepted of a Commiffion that is manifeftly illegal , and who have executed it contrary to all Law ; and that now one of their chief Members has abjured the *Proteftant Religion*, and declared himfelf a *Papift* ; by which he is become uncapable of holding any publick Employment. The faid Commiffioners have hitherto given fuch proof of their Submiffion to the Directions given them , that there is no reafon to doubt , but they will ftill continue to promote all fuch defigns as will be moft agreeable to them. And thofe Evil Counfellors take care to raife none to any Ecclefiaftical Dignities , but perfons that have no Zeal for the *Proteftant Religion*, and that now hide their unconcernednefs for it, under the fpecious pretence of *Moderation*. The faid Commiffioners have fufpended the Bifhop of *London*, only becaufe he refufed to obey an Order that was fent him, to fufpend a worthy Divine, without fomuch as citing him before him to make his own Defence, or obferving the common forms of Procefs. They have turned out a Prefident chofen by the Fellows of *Magdalen-College*, and afterwards all the Fellows of that College, without fo much as citing them before any Court that could take legal Cognizance of that Affair, or obtaining any Sentence againft them by a competent Judge. And

People of *Ifrael.* When he had brought them out of *Egypt* , they own'd this as a Title to Government, that he would have had, even without Divine Nomination. Such was *Cecrops* among the *Athenians*, and *Romulus* among the *Romans*, and other firft Kings in other Nations. *p.* 11, 12.

Next to thefe, and fomething like them, were the firft Planters of Colonies : Such as *Cadmus* was at *Thebes*, *Æneas* in *Latium*, and the like. In *England* fuch were *Hengift*, and the reft that began the Seven Kingdoms of the *Saxon* Heptarchy. From one of thefe , namely, from *Cerdic*, King of the *Weft-Saxons*, the Defcent of our Royal Family is unqueftionable. *But not in the Right Line , Sir , under favour.*

But the moft like to Founders are they whom God raifes up to be the Reftorers and Deliverers of a People, when they are either brought low by Tyranny and Oppreffion , or when they are torn in pieces by Factions among themfelves. *p.* 12,13.

Thus when the *Roman* State, being torn by a long Civil War, had even bled it felf to death, (it had certainly expir'd, if it had been left to it felf) *Auguftus* came in, and not only bound up the Wounds, but put, as it were, a new Soul into the Body ; He made it not only live, but flourifh, by his great Care and Wifdom, and Induftry ; which fo oblig'd the People, that they even forc'd him to accept of the Empire. Thefe were fuch Benefits to Mankind, as whofoever was enabled to do, it was

And the only reason that was given for turning them out, was their refufing to chufe for their Prefident, a perfon that was recommended to them, by the Inftigation of thofe Evil Counfellors, tho the Right of a Free Election belong'd undoubtedly to them. But they were turned out of their Free-holds contrary to Law, and to that exprefs provifion in the *Magna Charta*, *That no man fhall lofe Life or Goods, but by the Law of the Land.* And now thefe Evil Counfellors have put the faid College wholly into the hands of Papifts ; tho, as is abovefaid, they are incapable of all fuch Employments, both by the Law of the Land, and the Statutes of the College. Thefe Commiffioners have alfo cited before them all the Chancellors and Archdeacons of *England*, requiring them to certifie to them the Names of all fuch Clergy-men as have read the King's Declaration for *Liberty of Confcience* , and of fuch as have not read it, without confidering that the reading of it was not enjoyned the Clergy by the Bifhops who are their Ordinaries. The Illegality and Incompetency of the faid Court of the Eccleliaftical Commiffioners was fo notorioufly known, and it did fo evidently appear, that it tended to the Subverfion of the *Proteftant Religion*, that the moft Reverend Father in God, *William* Archbifhop of *Canterbury*, Primate and Metropolitan of all *England*, feeing that it was raifed for no other end, but to opprefs fuch perfons as were of eminent Virtue, Learn-

as if God had put a Glory about his Head ; it fo markt him out to the People, that they could not go befide him in their Choice ; they took him as one already chofen of God. *p.* 13. *No ; they took him as a fuccefsful Tyrant, whom they had not power to withftand. The* Romans *did not underftand our new-coin'd Choice of God. And if our Regency-men had known that the Prince of* Orange *was chofen of God, they would not have voted as they did.*

In thofe Kingdoms wherein the Succeffion is continued by a new Election upon every Vacancy, or wherein a new Election is made upon the Extinguifhing of the Royal Family, the perfon on whom the Election falls in either cafe, owes his promotion to God, from whom it comes the fame way to him, as it came to his firft Predeceffor in that Kingdom. *p.* 16.

In all forts of Government , as the Sovereign Power in every Countrey or Nation is of God, fo they that are invefted with it, whether one or many, are in the place of God, and have their *Promotion* from him.

The Transferring of this Power from one to another, is the Act of God. And this he does, proceeding Judicially, as being *Judge. p.* 17.

Firft, God does this : Secondly, He does it Judicially.

For the firft of thefe, God has fuch an Intereft in the difpofing of power, as none can pretend to but himfelf.

Men have their part in fetting up what

Learning and Piety, refufed to fit, or to concur in it.

8. And tho there are many exprefs Laws againft all Churches or Chappels for the exercife of the Popifh Religion, and alfo againft all Monafteries and Convents, and more particularly againft the Order of the *Jefuits*; yet thofe Evil Counfellors have procured orders for the building of feveral Churches and Chappels for the exercife of that Religion. They have alfo procured divers Monafteries to be erected, and in contempt of the Law, they have not only fet up feveral Colleges of *Jefuits* in divers places, for the corrupting of the Youth, but have raifed up one of the *Order* to be a Privy-Counfellor, and a Minifter of State. By all which they do evidently fhew, That they are reftrained by no rules of Law whatfoever, but that they have fubjected the Honours and Eftates of the Subjects, and the Eftablifh'd Religion, to a Defpotick Power, and to Arbitrary Government. In all which they are ferved and feconded by thofe Ecclefiaftical Commiffioners.

9. They have alfo followed the fame Methods with relation to Civil Affairs; for they have procured orders to examine all Lords Lieutenants, Deputy-Lieutenants, Sheriffs, Juftices of Peace, and all others that were in any publick Employment, if they would concur with the King in the Repeal of the *Teft* and *Penal Laws*, and all fuch whofe Confciences did not fuffer them to comply with their defigns, were turned out

what they cannot put down again. It is a Woman's Confent makes a Man be her Husband; the Fellows of a College chufe one to be their Head; a Corporation chufe one to be their Mayor: All thefe do only chufe the perfon, they do not give him the Authority. It is the Law that gives that, and that Law fo binds their hands, that they cannot undo what they have done.

No more can a Nation undo its own Act, in chufing Men into Sovereign power. I do not fay but they may chufe Men into Government, exprefly with that Condition, That they fhall be accountable to the people; and then the Government remains in the Body of the Nation, it is that which we properly call a Commonwealth. But for Sovereign Princes and Kings, even where they are chofen by the Nation; and much more in Hereditary Kingdoms; as they have their Authority from God, fo they are only accountable to him. For he is *the only Potentate, King of kings, and Lord of lords.* He alone both makes Kings by his Sovereign Power, and by the fame he can unmake them when he pleafes. *p.*18,19.

Nay, more than fo, *He puts down one, and fets up another.* Both the Words imply fomething of an high place, and here they are ufed of Civil Government or Dominion. Of this it is faid, That God fo deprives one of it, as that he advances another in his ftead.

This can be underftood of nothing elfe but the Conqueft of one Prince out, and others were put in their places, who, they believed, would be more compliant to them in their Designs of defeating the Intent and Execution of those Laws which had been made with so much care and caution for the security of the *Protestant Religion.* And in many of these places they have put profess'd Papists, tho the Law has disabled them, and warranted the Subjects not to have any regard to their Orders.

10. They have also invaded the Privileges, and seized on the Charters of most of those Towns that have a right to be represented by their Burgesses in Parliament, and have procured Surrenders to be made of them, by which the Magistrates in them have delivered up all their Rights and Privileges, to be disposed of at the pleasure of those Evil Counsellors, who have thereupon placed new Magistrates in those Towns, such as they can most entirely confide in; and in many of them they have put Popish Magistrates, notwithstanding the Incapacities under which the Law hath put them.

11. And whereas no Nation whatsoever can subsist without the administration of good and impartial Justice, upon which mens Lives, Liberties, Honours and Estates do depend, those Evil Counsellors have subjected these to an Arbitrary and Despotick Power: In the most important Affairs they have studied to discover before-hand the Opinions of the Judges, and have turned out such as they found would not conform themselves to their Intentions, and have

Prince over another. For what one resigns by a Voluntary Act, he is said to lay down, or to give it up to another. But *putting down* is the Act of a Superior, by which one's place is taken from him against his Will. Now God being the Superior that does this by the Act of his Providence, it must be such an Act as gives the Power from *one* against his Will, to *another* whom God is pleased to set up in his stead. Thus in giving *one* Prince a Conquest over *another*, he thereby puts one in Possession of the other's Dominions, he makes the other's Subjects become his Subjects, or his Slaves, accordingly as they come in upon Conditions, or at the Will of the Conqueror. In short, he giveth him the whole Right and Power of the other Prince. *p.* 18, 19, 20.

When those Kings, that living in a *settled Kingdom,* will not govern according to the Laws thereof; it is a breach of Faith, not only to their people, but to God also, where they are sworn to the observing of Laws. And though they are not therefore to be deposed by the people, yet they cannot escape the vengeance of God, who ordinarily punishes them with the natural effects of their Sin.

On the other hand, if a Prince will have no Law but his Will, if he tramples and oppresseth his people, their patience will not hold out always, they will at one time or other shew themselves to be but Men. At least they will have no heart to fight for their Oppressor. So that if have put others in their places, of whom they were more assured, without having any regard to their Abilities. And they have not stuck to raise even professed Papists to the Courts of Judicature, notwithstanding their Incapacity by Law; and that no regard is due to any Sentences flowing from them. They have carried this so far, as to deprive such Judges, who in the common administration of Justice,shewed that they were governed by their Consciences, and not by the Directions which the others gave them. By which it is apparent, that they design to render themselves the absolute Masters of the Lives, Honours and Estates of the Subjects, of what rank or dignity soever they may be; and that without having any regard either to the Equity of the Cause, or to the Consciences of the Judges, whom they will have to submit in all things to their own Will and Pleasure; hoping by such ways to intimidate those who are yet in Employment, as also such others, as they shall think fit,to put in the rooms of those whom they have turned out; and to make them see what they must look for, if they should at any time act in the least contrary to their good liking; and that no failings of that kind are pardoned in any Persons whatsoever. A great deal of Blood has been shed in many places of the Kingdom, by Judges governed by those Evil Counsellors, against all the Rules and Forms of Law, without so much as suffering the Persons that were accused to plead in their own Defence.   12. They

a Foreign Enemy breaks in upon him, he is gone without remedy, unless God interpose. But how can that be, when *God is Judge* himself? Should the Judge hinder the doing of Justice? It is God's Work that Foreigners come to do, *Howbeit he meaneth not so.* He means nothing, perhaps, but the satisfying of his own Lust. But though he knoweth it not; he is sent in God's Message; for which all things being prepared by Natural Causes, and God not hindering his own Work, but rather hastning it; no wonder that it succeeds, and that oftentimes very easily. *p.24,25.*

When it happens (as it doth sometimes, and that especially for the Sins of a Nation), that they come to be under weak or wicked Kings; even these they must not *resist*, God hath taught them otherwise. What then? Must they be left to the Wills of these Tyrants? Or of them that govern weak Kings, which is commonly worse? Must they endure all the load of Oppression that these will lay upon them? That is, For a few Mens pleasure, must a Nation be made miserable? This is far from God's design in the Institution of Government. He makes Kings his *Ministers for the good* of their People. If any will take that Office upon them, they must behave themselves accordingly. Otherwise, if they take it as given them only for themselves, it is such a breach of Trust, that God cannot but punish them for it. But how should he do this, so as that the   punish-

12. They have also, by putting the Administration of Justice in the hands of Papists, brought all the Matters of Civil Justice into great uncertainties; with how much Exactness and Justice soever that these Sentences may have been given. For since the Laws of the Land do not only exclude Papists from all Places of Judicature, but have put them under an Incapacity; none are bound to acknowledge, or to obey their Judgments, and all Sentences given by them are null and void of themselves: So that all Persons who have been cast in Tryals before such Popish Judges, may justly look on their pretended Sentences as having no more force than the Sentences of any private and unauthorised Person whatsoever. So deplorable is the Case of the Subjects, who are obliged to answer to such Judges, that must in all things stick to the Rules which are set them by those Evil Counsellors, who as they raised them up to those Employments, so can turn them out of them at pleasure; and who can never be esteemed Lawful Judges; so that all their Sentences are in the Construction of the Law, of no Force and Efficacy. They have likewise disposed of all Military Employments, in the same manner: For tho the Laws have not only excluded Papists from all such Employments, but have in particular provided, that they should be disarmed; yet they, in contempt of these Laws, have not only armed the Papists, but have likewise raised them up to the greatest

punishment may have its effect, in warning others not to transgress in like manner? He cannot do this better, than by making Men his Instruments in it. And therefore it is that God, tho he has infinite ways, yet commonly chuses to employ Men in this Service. He either finds them at home, that are *not afraid of the Power, as they ought to be*; or he brings them in from Foreign Countries, *Whistling for the Fly out of Egypt, or the Bee out of the land of Assyria*: In plain words, stirring up a *Pharaoh*, or a *Nebuchadnezzar* against them. God may employ such if he will, tho none is too good for this work, to execute his righteous Judgments. And when God doth his work by their hands, whatsoever the Instruments may be, the Cause being so just, and so evident as we have supposed; *All men that see it, will say, Doubtless there is a God that judges on the earth.*

In the way of *Justice*, God acts as a *Judge* between Two Sovereign Powers, when they bring their Causes before him; that is, when they make War upon one another. And when he seeth his time, that is, when he finds the Cause ripe for Judgment, if it proceeds so far, then he gives Sentence for him that is injur'd, against him that hath done the Injury. The effect of this Sentence is a just Conquest; and that is the other way in which God, proceeding judicially, *puts down one, and sets up another.*

But the Pr. of Orange was not a Sovereign Power; being dispossest of his Principality.

That

eft Military Truft, both by Sea and Land, and that Strangers as well as Natives, and *Irish* as well as *English*, that fo by thofe means, having rendred themfelves Mafters both of the Affairs of the Church, of the Government of the Nation, and of the Courts of Juftice, and fubjected them all to a Defpotick and Arbitrary Power, they might be in a capacity to maintain and execute their wicked Defigns, by the affiftance of the Army, and thereby to enflave the Nation.

13. The difmal effects of this Subverfion of the Eftablifhed Religion, Laws and Liberties in *England*, appear more evidently to us, by what we fee done in *Ireland*; where the whole Government is put in the Hands of Papifts, where all the Proteftant Inhabitants are under the daily fears of what may be juftly apprehended from the Arbitrary Power which is fet up there: which has made great numbers of them leave that Kingdom, and abandon their Eftates in it, remembring well that Cruel and Bloody Maffacre which fell out in that Ifland in the Year 1641.

14. Thofe Evil Counfellors have alfo prevailed with the King to declare in *Scotland*, That he is cloathed with *Abfolute Power*, and that all the Subjects are bound *to obey him without referve* : upon which he has affumed an Arbitrary Power both over the Religion and Laws of that Kingdom ; from all which it is apparent, what is to be looked for in *England*, as foon as matters are duly prepared for it. 15. Thofe

That this may be the better underftood, there are four things to be confider'd particularly.

Firft, That War is an Appeal to the Juftice of God.

Secondly, That none can be Parties to this, but they that are in Sovereign Power.

Thirdly, That to make it a juft War, there muft be a juft and fufficient Caufe.

Fourthly, That Conqueft in fuch a War, is a decifive Judgment of God, and gives *one* a Right to the Dominions that he has conquered from the *other*.

That War is an Appeal to God; this appears in the nature of the thing. *p.* 25, 26, 27, 28.

The Parties to this Appeal, are properly fuch as have no Superior but God. For them that have an earthly Superior, their Appeal lies to him as *God's Minifter, attending continually on this very thing. p.* 29.

Subjects have no Right to make War, without the leave of their Princes. For as God has given Princes the power of the Sword, fo he forbids it to Subjects, under a great Penalty, *They that take the Sword fhall perifh with the Sword.* And if he has not admitted them to be Parties in his Court, then it is certain that they cannot fue there ; or if they do, they can acquire no Right by it. There is an Original Nullity in all their Proceedings.

As none have right of making War, but they that are in Sovereign Power, fo neither is it given to them that they may make what ufe of

15. Thofe great and infufferable Oppreflions, and the open Contempt of all Law, together with the Apprehenfions of the fad Confequences that muft certainly follow upon it, have put the Subjects under great and juft Fears; and have made them look after fuch lawful Remedies as are allowed of in all Nations: yet all has been without effect. And thofe Evil Counfellors have endeavoured to make all Men apprehend the lofs of their Lives, Liberties, Honours, and Eftates, if they fhould go about to preferve themfelves from this Oppreffion, by Petition, Reprefentations, or other means authorifed by Law. Thus did they proceed with the Archbifhop of *Canterbury*, and the other Bifhops, who having offered a moft humble Petition to the King, in terms full of Refpect, and not exceeding the number limited by Law, in which they fet forth in fhort, the Reafons for which they could not obey that Order, which, by the Inftigation of thofe Evil Counfellors, was fent them, requiring them to appoint their Clergy to read in their Churches the Declaration for *Liberty of Confcience*; were fent to Prifon, and afterwards brought to a Tryal, as if they had been guilty of fome enormous Crime. They were not only obliged to defend themfelves in that purfuit, but to appear before profeffed Papifts, who had not taken the Teft, and by confequence were Men whofe Intereft led them to condemn them; and the Judges that gave their Opinion in their favours, were thereupon turned out. 16. And

of it they pleafe: Particularly, they muft not make War for the fatisfying of their Lufts, Ambition, Covetoufnefs, Vain-glory, or the like. Nay, the righteous God will not hold him guiltlefs that hath Juftice in his Caufe, and yet in his Heart hath no fuch thing. Lawful things muft be done lawfully. This Princes muft look to, as they will anfwer it to God.

But as far as man can judge, it is a Lawful War that is made for a juft and fufficient Caufe. *p.* 32. 33.

One Prince may make War in defence of another King's Subjects, if they fee themfelves in extreme danger of fuffering an intolerable Injury by his Oppreffion of his own people. And in thefe cafes, if one Lawfully may, then it is certain he ought to do it. *p.* 36.

They are fo much the more obliged to this, when it is evident, that the threatning mifchief is like to fall upon others, as well as themfelves; and them, fuch as they are bound in Honour and Confcience to protect and fupport. When by fitting ftill they fhould certainly expofe, not only themfelves to be ruined, but alfo their Friends and Allies to perifh with them; in that cafe, *Sævitia eft voluiffe mori*, it is a fort of bloody Peaceablenefs, it is cruelty to Mankind to go to that degree of fuffering Injuries.

But efpecially, when the Caufe of God is concern'd, to whom we owe all things, and ought to venture all for his fake. Surely 'tis his Caufe, when it touches Religion; which is all

16. And yet it cannot be pretended, that any Kings, how great soever their Power has been, and how Arbitrary and Defpotick foever they have been in the exercife of it, have ever reckoned it a Crime for their Subjects to come in all Submiffion and Refpect, and in a due number, not exceeding the limits of the Law, and reprefent to them the Reafons that made it impoffible for them to obey their Orders. Thofe Evil Counfellors have alfo treated a Peer of the Realm as a Criminal, only becaufe he faid, That the Subjects were not bound to obey the Orders of a Popifh Juftice of Peace; though it is evident, that they being by Law rendred incapable of all fuch Trufts, no regard is due to their Order. This being the fecurity which the People have by the Law for their Lives, Liberties, Honours and Eftates, That they are not to be fubjected to the Arbitrary Proceedings of Papifts, that are contrary to Law, put into any Employment Civil or Military.

17. Both We our felves, and our Deareft and moft Entirely Beloved Confort the Princefs, have endeavoured to fignify, in terms full of refpect to the King, the juft and deep Regret which all thefe Proceedings have given us; and in Compliance with his Majefty's Defires fignified to us, We declared both by Word of Mouth, to his Envoy, and in Writing, what our Thoughts were touching the Repealing of the *Teft and Penal Laws*; which we did in fuch a manner, that we

all that is dear to him in this world. And tho Religion it felf teaches us, *if it be poffible, as much as in us lies, to live peaceably with all men*; yet as 'tis there fuppofed, there may be Caufe to break the Peace; fo it adds infinitely to that Caufe, when it comes to concern our Religion. *p.*36, 37.

There is yet a greater Caufe for this, when the Suffering-Religion is that which is eftablifh'd by the Laws of that Kingdom; and yet the King that is fworn to thofe Laws, and therefore bound to fupport that Religion, is manifeftly practifing againft it, and endeavours to fupplant, and opprefs, and extinguifh it. What fhould other Princes or States that profefs the fame Religion, do in this cafe? They fee that fuch a King is fet upon the deftroying of their Religion. He hath declar'd a hoftile mind towards the profeffors of it, in judging them not capable of enjoying their Temporal Rights. If he deals thus with his own People, what are Foreigners to expect at his hands? Can they think themfelves fecure, becaufe they are at peace with him? They cannot; unlefs Treaties are more Sacred than Laws. Or can they rely upon his Oath? But they fee he hath broken it. And therefore they have reafon to judge, That either he makes no Confcience of an Oath, or he thinks Faith is not to be kept with Hereticks, or he hath a Superior that can difpenfe with him, or that will abfolve him from the guilt of Perjury in fuch cafes where Religion is concerned. In fhort, they are fure of his we hoped we had propofed an Expedient by which the Peace of thofe Kingdoms, and a happy Agreement among the Subjects of all Perfuafions, might have been fetled : but thofe Evil Counfellors have put fuch ill Conftructions on thefe our good Intentions, that they have endeavoured to alienate the King more and more from us ; as if We had defigned to difturb the Quiet and Happinefs of the Kingdom.

18. The laft and great Remedy for all thofe Evils, is *the calling of a Parliament,* for fecuring the Nation againft the evil Practices of thofe wicked Counfellors: But this could not be yet compaffed, nor can it be eafily brought about. For thofe Men apprehending, that a Lawful Parliament being once affembled, they would be brought to an account for all their open Violations of Law, and for their Plots and Confpiracies againft the Proteftant Religion, and the Lives, and Liberties of the Subject, they have endeavoured, under the fpecious Pretence of *Liberty of Confcience,* firft to fow Divifions among Proteftants, between thofe of the *Church of England* and the *Diffenters:* The defign being laid to engage Proteftants, that are all equally concerned, to preferve themfelves from Popifh Oppreffion, into mutual Quarrellings, that fo by thefe, fome Advantages might be given to them to bring about their Defigns ; and that both in the Election of the Members of Parliament, and afterwards in the Parliament it felf. For they fee

his Will to deftroy them, and cannot be fure of his Oath to the contrary. Wherein then can they be fafe ? But in his want of power to do them hurt ? But he will not want power, if they let him go on, for he is getting it as faft as he can. He is now ftrengthning himfelf by thofe ways that he takes to be abfolute Lord of his own people : And he is now weakning Them, by oppreffing all thofe among his people, whom he knows to be their Friends and Well-wifhers. He doth both thefe things together : He daily leffens their party, and makes them as many more Enemies, as he gains Men over to his Religion. And if that be fuch a Religion as pretends to a Right of deftroying Men of other Religions ; knowing this, they know what they are to expect. When this pretended Right is armed with power, it will certainly fall upon them. So that they muft begin before he is ready for them, or elfe it will be too late to do any thing for their own prefervation.

But as it is neceffary for them to do this for themfelves, fo they ought to do it much the rather for the fakes of their oppreffed Brethren : That, by a timely afferting of their own Right, they may alfo deliver them from the Evils they fuffer at prefent, and fave them from that Deftruction which is coming upon them. As it was juft and neceffary on thofe former Accounts, fo this makes it a pious Caufe, and therefore the more worthy of a true well, that if all Proteſtants could enter into a mutual good underſtanding one with another, and concur together in the preſerving of their Religion, it would not be poſſible for them to compaſs their wicked Ends. They have alſo required all Perſons in the ſeveral Counties of *England*, that either were in any Employment, or were in any conſiderable Eſteem, to declare before-hand that they would concur in the Repeal of the *Teſt and Penal Laws* ; and that they would give their Voices in the Elections to Parliament, only for ſuch as would concur in it ; ſuch as would not thus preingage themſelves, were turned out of all Employments; And others who entred into thoſe Engagements, were put into their places, many of them being Papiſts : And contrary to the Charters and Privileges of thoſe Burroughs that have a Right to ſend Burgeſſes to Parliament, they have ordered ſuch Regulations to be made, as they thought fit and neceſſary, for aſſuring themſelves of all the Members that are to be choſen by thoſe Corporations : and by this means they hope to avoid that Puniſhment which they have deſerved ; tho it is apparent, that all Acts made by Popiſh Magiſtrates are null and void of themſelves : So that no Parliament can be Lawful, for which the Elections and Returns are made by Popiſh Sheriffs and Mayors of Towns ; and therefore as long as the Authority and Magiſtracy is in ſuch hands, it is not poſſible to have any Lawful Parliament. And tho according

Chriſtian Prince. It has been judg'd ſo by them whoſe Names we have in great Veneration. We have the Examples of our own Princes here in *England*, in the beſt of Times ſince the Reformation : Theſe the Reader may find collected to his hand, in an excellent Book that hath been lately publiſhed. But this may as well be ſhewn in the Examples of them whom our Princes choſe to follow as their Paterns ; namely, of the Chriſtians in Primitive Times, and eſpecially at the time of the firſt *Nicene* Council. In theſe times we find that *Conſtantine* and *Licinius*, having ſhar'd the *Roman* Empire between them, had paſſed a Decree together at *Milan*, for Chriſtianity to be the Eſtabliſhed Religion : And when afterward *Licinius*, in his part of the Empire, would have oppreſs'd it contrary to Law ; for that cauſe *Conſtantine* the Great made War upon him ; and in proſecution of that War, thruſt him out of his Empire : For which he was ſo far from being blamed by any Chriſtian in thoſe times, even by thoſe that had been *Licinius*'s Subjects, as moſt of thoſe Biſhops were, that ſate in the *Nicene* Council, that they all gave him the higheſt Praiſes and Encomiums, and bleſſed God that had ſent them that happy Deliverance by his means. *Euſebius* was *Licinius*'s Subject, and he afterwards writ the Life of *Conſtantine* the Great, in which they that pleaſe may read whole Chapters to this purpoſe.

As

cording to the Conftitution of the *Englifh* Government, and Immemorial Cuftom, all Elections of Parliament-men ought to be made with an entire Liberty, without any fort of Force, or the requiring the Electors to chufe fuch Perfons as fhall be named to them ; and the Perfons thus freely elected, ought to give their Opinions freely, upon all Matters that are brought before them, having the good of the Nation ever before their eyes, and following in all things the Dictates of their Confcience ; yet now the People of *England* cannot expect a Remedy from a *Free Parliament*, legally called and chofen. But they may perhaps fee one called, in which all Elections will be carried by Fraud or Force, and which will be compofed of fuch Perfons, of whom thofe Evil Counfellors hold themfelves well affured, in which all things will be carried on according to their Direction and Intereft, without any regard to the Good or Happinefs of the Nation ; which may appear evidently from this, that the fame Perfons tried the Members of the laft Parliament, to gain them to Confent to the Repeal of the *Teft and Penal Laws*, and procured that Parliament to be diffolved, when they found that they could not, neither by Promifes nor Threatnings, prevail with the Members to comply

As that is a juft War which is made upon juft and fufficient Caufe, fo the Effect of fuch a War, being a Conqueft, is Juft.

Conqueft being the way by which a Kingdom or Dominion is taken from a Sovereign Prince againft his Will, and by which another Prince gets it into his Poffeffion ; as often as this happens, there arifes a Queftion between the two Princes, whether of them hath a Right to that Kingdom or Dominion.

For the deciding of this Queftion, it muft be by fuch a Law as is common to both the Parties, whofe Rights are to be judg'd by it. That cannot be the Law of the Kingdom ; for tho the Prince that is diffeiz'd, was obliged by that Law while he was in poffeffion, yet now it feems he is not ; and it never was a Law to the Prince that is now in his place. It muft therefore be a Superior Law, fuch as is common to all Sovereign Princes in their Affairs with one another, and that (as hath been already fhewn) is ordinarily the Law of Nations.

I fay ordinarily, becaufe there is yet a Superior Law, namely, the Law of God ; whether written in our Hearts, which we commonly call the Law of Nature ; or whether an exprefs Revelation from God, fuch as was fometimes given time for the effecting of them, for the encouraging of their Complices, and for the difcouraging of all good Subjects, have publifhed, That the *Queen* hath brought forth a *Son* ; though there have appeared both during the *Queen's* pretended bignefs,and in the manner in which the Birth was managed, fo many juft and vifible grounds of Sufpicion, that not only we our felves, but all the good Subjects of thofe Kingdoms, do vehemently fufpect, that the pretended Prince of *Wales* was not born by the *Queen.* And it is notorioufly known to all the World, that many both doubted of the *Queen's* Bignefs, and of the birth of the Child, and yet there was not any one thing done to fatisfie them, or to put an end to their Doubts.

20. And fince our Deareft and moft Entirely beloved Confort the Princefs, and likewife We Our Selves, have fo great an Intereft in this Matter,and fuch a Right,as all the World knows, to the Succeffion to the Crown : Since alfo the *Englifh* did in theYear 1672.when theStates General of the *United Provinces* were invaded in a moft unjuft War, ufe their utmoft endeavours to put an end to that War, and that in oppofition to thofe who were then in the Government; and by their fo doing, they ran the hazard of lofing both the Favour of the Court, and their employments: and fince the *Englifh* Nation has ever teftified a moft particular Affection and Efteem, both to our Deareft Confort the Princefs, and to Our felves,
We

But whether, or how far, this may alter the cafe, will be confidered afterwards; at prefent we are only to confider what Judgment can be made of it, according to the Law of Nations.

By this it feems to be plain, That the Right fhould go along with the compleat poffeffion : So as that wherefoever this is once fettled, whether by length of time, or even fooner, by a general Confent of the people, there it ought to be prefumed there is a Right, at leaft, there ought to be no farther Difpute of it. There feems to be the fame reafon for this, that there is for the Law of Nations it felf; for if that Law was ordained for the peace of mankind, this quitting of poffeffion muft be a part of it,for there can be no end of Wars otherwife. *p.*45,46,47,to 51.

This appears by *Jephtha's* Speech to the King of *Ammon* that had *Chemofh* for his God ; *Wilt not thou poffefs that which* Chemofh *thy God giveth thee to poffefs? So whomfoever the Lord our God fhall drive out from before us, them will we poffefs. p.* 51.

It is by way of Conqueft, that God *puts down one, and fets up another.* For fo the *Babylonian* Empire was put down by *Cyrus,* who fet up the *Perfian* in its ftead. The *Perfian* Empire was put down in their laft King *Darius,* and *Alexander* fet up the *Macedon* in its ftead. The *Macedon* Kingdom was put down in their laft King *Perfeus,* and the *Roman* was fet up in its ftead.

All thefe Kingdoms were changed by Conquefts that they made
one

We cannot excuse our selves from Espousing their Interests, in a Matter of such high Consequence; and from contributing all that lies in us, for the maintaining both of the *Protestant Religion*, and of the Laws and Liberties of those Kingdoms, and for the Securing to them the continual enjoyment of all their just Rights. To the doing of which, We are most earnestly solicited by a great many Lords, both Spiritual and Temporal,and by many Gentlemen and other Subjects of all Ranks.

21. Therefore it is, that We have thought fit to go over to *England*, and to carry over with us a Force, sufficient by the Blessing of God, to defend us from the Violence of those Evil Counsellors. And We being desirous that our Intentions in this may be rightly understood, have for this end prepared this *Declaration*, in which, as we have hitherto given a True Account of the Reasons inducing us to it; so we now think fit to declare, That this our Expedition is intended for no other design, but to have a Free and Lawful Parliament Assembled, as soon as is possible: And that in order to this, all the late Charters by which the Elections of Burgesses are limited contrary to the Ancient Custom, shall be considered as null and of no force: And likewise all Magistrates who have been unjustly turned out, shall forthwith resume their former employments, as well as all the Burroughs of *England* shall return again to their Ancient Prescriptions and

one upon another. And so it was by those Conquests, that God *removed Kings, and set up Kings. p. 53*.

I do not say but they would have opposed the making of one of those Conquests, namely, that of *Alexander* the Great, because King *Darius* was then living. But when they saw they could not Oppose, the Conquest being already made, then Just or Unjust, they submitted to it; and having submitted, they were subject without any more Controversie.

Therefore also Just and Religious Kings have reckoned their Conquests among the great things that God wrought by their means; and accounted them as much their Subjects whom they had gain'd by the Sword, as them that were born in their Dominions.

Therefore also God hath commanded his people to give Obedience to the Kings that came in by Conquest, without any other Title. Nay, to such as were capable of no other; for they were forbidden *to set a stranger over them, which was not their brother*. And yet they were Subjects to strangers, such as *Cushan*, *Eglon*, and *Jabin*, &c. And in *Zedekiah*'s time God commanded them upon pain of death, to become the Subjects of *Nebuchadnezzar*, who had made a full Conquest over them, and held their lawful King *Jeconiah* then in Captivity. This is plainly the Doctrine of that Convocation which sate in the beginning of King *James* I. his time; and therefore it cannot but be very unjust, to charge

any

and Charters; and more particularly, that the Ancient Charter of the Great and Famous City of *London* , shall again be in force: And that the Writs for the Members of Parliament shall be addressed to the proper Officers, according to Law and Custom. That also none be suffered to chuse, or to be chosen Members of Parliament, but such as are qualified by Law: And that the Members of Parliament being thus lawfully Chosen, they shall meet and sit in full Freedom ; that so the two Houses may concur in the preparing of such Laws, as they upon full and free Debate shall judge necessary and convenient, both for the confirming and executing the Law concerning the *Test*, and such other Laws as are necessary for the security and maintenance of the *Protestant Religion*; as likewise for making such Laws as may establish a good agreement between the *Church of England* and all *Protestant Dissenters*; as also for the covering and securing of all such who will live peaceably under the Government, as becomes good Subjects, from all persecution upon the account of their Religion, even *Papists* themselves not excepted ; and for the doing of all other things, which the Two Houses of Parliament shall find necessary for the Peace, Honour and Safety of the Nation, so that there may be no more danger of the Nations falling at any time hereafter under *Arbitrary Government*. To this Parliament we will also refer theEnquiry into the Birth of the pretended Prince

any Man with Singularity or Novelty, that goes in the steps of so many and so great Authors. *p.* 53, 54, 55.

But some Learned and Judicious Men think, That whereas an unjust Conquest happens through the Judgment of God, for the punishing of a sinful Prince or Nation ; it doth not appear that he that is the Instrument of this, acquires any Right by it ; more than those Pirates or Robbers, who are instrumental likewise, in the punishing of inferior Transgressors. And if God gives no Right to him whom he sets up, then it remains still in him whom he has put down: So that he is rightful King still, tho he is out of possession, and the other is but an Usurper that is in possession.

In this case, if the Usurper has no pretence of Right, no prescription of Time , no Consent of the people, but only an unjust possession; how a Subject ought to behave himself towards him, even this is a *Difficult Question* , in a most learned Man's Judgment : Who yet judges, That even here it may be not only Lawful, but a Duty, to obey him that is in possession, when the Legal King is reduced to that pass, that he can no more do the Office of a King to his people. For (saith he) the Kingdom cannot be without Government; and if the Usurper preserves the Kingdom, a Lover of his Countrey ought not (as things are) to give any further cause of trouble by his unprofitable Contumacy. But then put case the Usurper hath sworn the people to him, and doth

Prince of *Wales*, and of all things relating to it, and to the Right of Succeſſion.

22. And We, for our part, will concur in every thing that may procure the Peace and Happineſs of the Nation, which a Free and Lawful Parliament ſhall determine; ſince we have nothing before our Eyes in this our undertaking, but the preſervation of the *Proteſtant Religion*, the Covering of all men from perſecution for their Conſciences, and the ſecuring to the whole Nation the free enjoyment of all their Laws, Rights and Liberties, under a Juſt and Legal Government.

23. This is the Deſign that we have propoſed to our ſelves, in appearing upon this occaſion in Arms: In the Conduct of which, We will keep the Forces under our Command, under all the ſtrictneſs of Martial Diſcipline; and take a ſpecial care, that the people of the Countries through which we muſt March, ſhall not ſuffer by their means; and as ſoon as the ſtate of the Nation will admit of it, We promiſe that we will ſend back all thoſe Foreign Forces that We have brought along with us.

24. We do therefore hope that all people will judge rightly of us, and approve of theſe our proceedings: But We chiefly rely on the Bleſſing of God for the Succeſs of this our Undertaking, in which We place our whole and only Confidence.

25. We do in the laſt place invite and require all perſons whatſoever,

doth the Office of a King, which (it ſeems) in his Judgment doth not take away the duty that is owing to that former King; how one can pay his duty to both, the expell'd Legal King, and to ſuch an Uſurper. This our Author ſays is *a moſt difficult Scruple*; and ſo it ſeems both by his, and our moſt Learned Caſuiſt's handling the Queſtion; where they ſhew how far one ought, and how far one ought not to comply with ſuch an Uſurpation. *p.* 56, 57, 58.

But theſe Difficulties are only in caſe the poſſeſſion is obtained by a War that was certainly unjuſt; for if the cauſe of the War was but doubtful, and a Conqueſt follows upon it, there is no place for theſe difficulties: Much leſs where the cauſe of War was certainly Juſt; for if a Conqueſt follows upon this, it gives a Right, and then there is no Uſurpation.

It has been commonly judg'd by the Law of Nations, That the Right goes along with the Poſſeſſion. Of this we ſee Examples in every Revolution that happens in this or any other Kingdom. When a King is driven out with any colour of Right, the Neighbouring Princes and States make no great difficulty of applying themſelves to him that comes in his ſtead; wherein though perhaps they too much follow their own Intereſt, yet it cannot be ſaid that what they do is againſt the Law of Nations. But what ſhould Subjects do in this Caſe? Of this we have an Example in the People of God, when they paſs'd ever, all the Peers of the Realm both Spiritual and Temporal, all Lords Lieutenants, Deputy-Lieutenants, and all Gentlemen, Citizens, and other Commons of all ranks, to come and assist us, in order to the Executing of this our Design, against all such as shall endeavour to Oppose us; that so we may prevent all those Miseries which must needs follow upon the Nations being kept under Arbitrary Government and Slavery: And that the Violences and Disorders which have overturned the whole Constitution of the *English* Government, may be fully redressed in a *Free and Legal Parliament.*

26. And we do likewise resolve, that as soon as the Nations are brought to a state of Quiet, We will take care that a Parliament shall be called in *Scotland,* for the restoring the Ancient Constitution of that Kingdom, and for bringing the Matters of Religion to such a Settlement, that the people may live easie and happy, and for putting an end to all the unjust Violences, that have been in a course of so many years committed there.

We will also study to bring the Kingdom of *Ireland* to such a state, that the Settlement there may be religiously observed; and that the Protestant and British Interest there, may be secured. And we will endeavour by all possible means, to procure such an Establishment in all the Three Kingdoms, that they may all live in a happy Union and Correspondence together; and that the

pass'd successively under the Yoke of those Four great Monarchs that were formerly mention'd. It is likely that each of those Kings that got the Power over them, first declar'd the Cause of the War that he made upon the former Lords. In that Case, though they could not judge of the Cause, whether it was Just or Unjust, yet no doubt they did well in adhering to him that was in present Possession. *p.* 60,61.

To a People that are in such a case, it is no small Comfort, that whatsoever doubt they may have of the Cause of the War, yet there is no doubt at all concerning their Duty. There is nothing more certain than this, that they ought to preserve themselves, if they can do it lawfully. But it is lawful for them to forbear fighting, when they are unsatisfied of the Cause: And if their own Prince is not able to protect them, it is lawful for them to take protection elsewhere. Therefore in case of Invasion for a Cause which is just, for ought they know, it is lawful for them to live quietly under the Invader: nay, it is not only lawful, but their duty (as hath been already shewn) to acquiesce in his Government, when he comes to be in Possession.

But when they are certain that a War is made upon their Prince for just Cause; that is, when they plainly see he hath drawn it upon himself, by making it not only lawful, but necessary for another Prince to invade him for his own Preservation; What are the People to do in this the Proteſtant Religion, and the Peace, Honour and Happineſs of thoſe Nations, may be eſtabliſhed upon laſting Foundations.

Given under our Hand and Seal, at our Court in the Hague, *the Tenth day of* October, *in the year of our Lord,* 1688.

William Henry, Prince of *Orange.*

By his Highneſs ſpecial Command,

C. Huygens,

The King having received advice that the preparations in *Holland* were deſigned for *England*, caſt about how to prevent the Peoples running to joyn with the Prince: In order to which he was adviſed to appeaſe them, by ſeeming to ſtep backward, and undo ſome things that he knew had given a general diſtaſte againſt his Government. Hereupon the Eccleſiaſtical Commiſſion was taken away, the Biſhop of *London* and the Maſter and Fellows of *Magdalen-College* reſtored; as likewiſe the Ancient Charters of Cities and Boroughs, and a Free Parliament promiſed to be called, when the Kingdom ſhould be freed from a Foreign Force.

This occaſioned the Prince to publiſh his Additional Declaration.

His Highneſs's additional Declaration, &c.

AFter we had Prepared and Printed this our Declartion, We

this Caſe? No doubt they ought firſt to have a care of their Souls, and not to endanger them by being Partakers of other mens Sins. They cannot but ſee, that, by engaging in the War, they abet their own Prince in his Injuſtice; though not in his doing the Injury, yet in continuing what is done, and in his not giving Reparation. And therefore they are ſubject to the ſame puniſhment with him. Nay their Condition is worſe than his: For he may ſhift for himſelf, and leave them, and all they have, to be a Prey to the Enemy: Who by right of War may do with them and theirs what he pleaſes. It is therefore certainly their wiſeſt Courſe to keep themſelves free from all offence, both towards God, and towards Man: That having had no part in the Cauſe of the War, they may not be involv'd in the ill Conſequences of it. And this they have reaſon to expect from a Generous Enemy, that he will not uſe the Right of War againſt them that deſire to live peaceably. Much more, if he hath declar'd he would not hurt them that ſhould not reſiſt him, they have reaſon to truſt a juſt Prince upon his Declaration. And if he went ſo far as to declare, That upon their Submiſſion they ſhould enjoy the benefit of their own Laws; then, although it ſhould come to a Conqueſt, they may reaſonably expect to be in no worſe condition under the Stranger, than they were under their own Prince: They have his Faith engaged to them for this.

But

We have underſtood that the Sub-verters of the Religion and Laws of thoſe Kingdoms, hearing of Our Preparations to aſſiſt the People a-gainſt them, have begun to retract ſome of the Arbitrary and Deſpo-tick Powers that they had aſſumed, and to vacate ſome of their Injuſt Judgments and Decrees. The ſenſe of their Guilt, and the diſtruſt of their Force, have induced them to offer to the City of *London* ſome ſeeming Relief from their great Oppreſſions; hoping thereby to quiet the People, and to divert them from demanding a Re-eſta-bliſhment of their Religion and Laws under the ſhelter of our Arms: They do alſo give out, That we do intend to Conquer and En-ſlave the Nation; and therefore it is that we have thought fit to add a few words to our Declaration.

We are confident, that no Per-ſons can have ſuch hard thoughts of us, As to imagine that we have any other Deſign in this Undertaking, than to procure a Settlement of the Religion, and of the Liberties and Properties of the Subjects upon ſo ſure a Foundation, that there may be no danger of the Nations relapſing into the like Miſeries at any time hereafter. And as the Forces that we have brought along with us, are utterly diſproportioned to that wicked Deſign of Conque-ring the Nation, if we were capa-ble of Intending it; ſo the great numbers of the Principal Nobility and Gentry, that are Men of Emi-nent Quality and Eſtates, and Per-

ſons

But if the Stranger declares he makes War in defence of another King's Subjects, as (we have ſhewn) he may lawfully do, when he finds himſelf in danger of ſuffering by that King's Oppreſſion of his own People; in this Caſe, they are firſt to conſider, whether it is a mere pretence, or whether there be a real ground for his Declaration. If they find there is a juſt and ſufficient ground for it, they ſee in effect, that it is through Them that he is ſtruck at; and therefore the War is not ſo much His, as their own. It is true according to our Doctrine, they are united to their Prince as a Wife to her Husband; ſo that they can no more right themſelves by Arms, than ſhe can ſue her Husband while the Bond of Marriage conti-nues. Yet as, When her Husband uſes her extremely ill, ſhe may com-plain of him to the Judge, who, if he ſees Cauſe, may diſſolve the Marriage by his Sentence; and after that ſhe is at liberty to ſue him as well as any other Man: So a Peo-ple may cry to the Lord by reaſon of their Oppreſſion, and he may raiſe them up a Deliverer, that ſhall take the Government into his hands (a Foreign Prince may law-fully do this, as hath been already ſhewn) and then they are not only free to defend themſelves, but are oblig'd to join with him, againſt their Oppreſſor. *p.* 62, 63, 64, 65.

In this Caſe, if another Prince, having a juſt Cauſe of War, is ſo far concern'd for ſuch a People, as to take them into his Care, and to de-

clare

fons of known Integrity and Zeal both for the Religion and Government of *England*, many of them being alfo diftinguifhed by their conftant Fidelity to the Crown, who do both accompany us in this Expedition, and have earneftly folicited us to it, will cover us from all fuch malicious Infinuations: For it is not to be imagin'd, that either thofe who have Invited us, or thofe that are already come to Affift us, can join in a wicked attempt of Conqueft, to make void their own lawful Titles to their Honours, Eftates, and Interefts. We are alfo confident, that all Men fee how little weight there is to be laid on all Promifes and Engagements, that can be now made ; fince there has been fo little regard had in the time paft, to the moft folemn Promifes. And as that imperfect Redrefs that is now offered, is a plain Confeffion of thofe Violations of the Government that we have fet forth ; fo the Defectivenefs of it is no lefs apparent : For they lay down nothing which they may not take up at pleafure ; and they referve entire, and not fo much as mentioned, their Claims and Pretences to an Arbitrary and Defpotick Power ; which has been the Root of all their Oppreffion, and of the total Subverfion of the Government. And it is plain, that there can be no Redrefs nor Remedy offered but in Parliament ; by a Declaration of the Rights of the Subjects, that have been invaded, and not by any pretended Acts of Grace, to which the extremity of their Affairs has

clare that he makes the War for their Deliverance : The effect of this War, though we may call it a Conqueft, becaufe it has refemblance of it, yet it cannot be properly fo in any refpect ; whether we confider the Prince on whom it is made, or the People that have their Deliverance by it.

As to him, it is properly an *Eviction* by the juft Sentence of God ; who thus puts him out of a Truft, that he abufed, to the hurt of them for whofe fakes it was given him. And as to the people, it cannot be a Conqueft over them, who are fo far from having the War made againft them, that it was made chiefly for their fakes. If there be any pretence of a Conqueft, it is only over them that were their Oppreffors. *p. 66, 67.*

An Anfwer to Mr. Afhton's Paper, &c.

THE Matter in difpute is not whether *Rightful*, *Lawful Kings are to be obeyed*, but who in our prefent Circumftances is our Rightful, Lawful Sovereign ; not whether *Kings be not God's Vicegerents*, but whether God doth not fometimes confer the Right of Sovereignty by a *Law fuperiour* to the *Laws of particular Countries*, that is, by the *Law of Nations*, which eftablifheth fuch a *Right* upon the fuccefs of a Juft War ; not *whether Sovereign Princes are not accountable only to God*, but whether Allegiance be

E

has driven them. Therefore it is that we have thought fit to declare, That we will refer all to a Free Assembly of the Nation, in a Lawful Parliament.

Given under our Hand and Seal, at our Court in the Hague, *the Twenty fourth day of* October, *in the year of our Lord,* 1688.

William Henry, *Prince of* Orange.

By his Highness's special Command,
C. Huygens.

Pursuant to the Peoples Invitation, and to carry on the ends of the foregoing Declaration, the Prince set Sail from *Holland,* with betwixt Four and Five Hundred Capital Ships, Fire-Ships, Pinks, and Tenders: And upon the Fifth of *November* landed in *Torbay* in *Devonshire.*

The people in great Numbers welcom'd his Highness with loud Acclamations of Joy. His Army consisted of about 15000 Horse and Foot.

After the Army was landed, and the Prince come to *Exeter,* the Gentry from all parts of *Devonshire, Somersetshire,* &c. flock'd to him in great numbers, few absenting themselves. Several of the Nobility came to him likewise, whilst in and about *Exeter*; others afterwards, when he was farther advanced towards *London.*

Before his Royal Highness left *Exeter,* there was an Association drawn up, and signed by all the Lords

be not due where the Rights of Sovereignty are placed, by an *extraordinary Act of Providence,* and the *concurrent Consent of the Nation.* p. 9, 10.

We must of necessity look back to the Occasions of this great Revolution: And there were two principal Occasions of it.

First, Great and violent Presumptions of an Injury to the Right of Succession.

Secondly, Too great Evidences of a formed Design to subvert the Established Religion and Civil Liberties of the Nation.

Now there are two very material Questions which arise from hence.

First, Whether these were the *just Occasions* of a War.

Secondly, Whether upon the success of this War, the *Rights of Sovereignty* were duly transferred?

If these were *just Occasions* of a War, and upon the Success thereof the *Sovereignty* was duly transferred, then there can be no Dispute left, to whom our Allegiance is due.

It is taken for granted by all who understand these Matters, That as there is a *Law of Nature,* which determines the Rights and Properties of particular Nations; and that all private Persons are bound to submit to the Municipal Laws of those Societies for their Peace and Security: So there are other Laws which concern those *Nations,* as they make up several *independent Governments* upon each other. And there are several Rights

Lords and Gentlemen that were with him, in these words; *viz.*

WE whose Names are hereunto subscribed, who have now joyned with the Prince of *Orange,* for the defence of the Proteſtant Religion, and for the maintaining the Ancient Government, and the Laws and Liberties of *England, Scotland,* and *Ireland,* do engage to Almighty God, to his Highneſs the Prince of *Orange,* and to one another, to ſtick firm to this Cauſe, and to one another, in the defence of it, and never to depart from it, until our Religion, Laws, and Liberties are ſo far ſecured to us in a Free Parliament, that we ſhall be no more in danger of falling under *Popery* and *Slavery.* And whereas we are engaged in this common Cauſe, under the Protection of the Prince of *Orange,* by which in caſe his Perſon may be expoſed to danger, and to the curſed attempts of *Papiſts,* and other bloody men; we do therefore ſolemnly engage to God and one another, That if any ſuch attempt be made upon him, we will purſue not only thoſe who make it, but all their Adherents, and all that we find in Arms againſt us, with the utmoſt ſeverity of a juſt Revenge, to their Ruin and Deſtruction. And that the execution of any ſuch Attempt (which God of his Infinite Mercy forbid) ſhall not divert us from proſecuting this Cauſe which we do now undertake, but that it ſhall engage us to carry it on with all the rigor that ſo barbarous a Practice ſhall deſerve. A-

Rights which belong to them with reſpect to one another, which do not belong to private Perſons as they live in ſubjection to any particular Government.

And as there are ſuch Rights, ſo there muſt be a juſt and lawful way for reparation of Injuries. In particular Governments, the thing is plain by Eſtabliſhed Laws and Courts of Judicature, whoſe Sentence is executed by the Civil Power; but in Separate Nations, and Independent Governments, although there be Laws by conſent, called the *Law of Nations;* yet there is no common Judicature to determine of Right and Wrong; and therefore in caſe of Injury, there is an allowance for the injured Party by this *Law of Nations* to right himſelf by force, as there would be to every particular Perſon, if there were no Laws nor Power to ſee them executed.

There is then a Right in every Sovereign and Independent Prince to exerciſe Force againſt another Prince, who detains any Right from him, or doth any Injury to him, or to thoſe he is bound to defend.

The Queſtion then comes to the *Juſt Occaſions* of ſuch a War; and here are two aſſigned.

Firſt, Great and violent Preſumptions of an Injury to the Right of Succeſſion. This is expreſly mentioned and inſiſted on, in the Declaration of the then Prince of *Orange* (our preſent King.) *p.* 9, 10, 11.

E 2 There

About this time a Printed Letter was difperfed amongft the Army, directed to the Officers, and inviting them to join with the Prince in the Deliverance of their Countrey.

Gentlemen and Friends,

WE have given you fo full and fo true an Account of our Intentions in this Expedition, in our *Declaration*, that as we can add nothing to it, fo we are fure you can defire nothing more of us. We are come to preferve your Religion, and to reftore and eftablifh your Liberties and Properties ; and therefore we cannot fuffer our felves to doubt, but that all true Englifh-men will come and concur with us in our defire to fecure thefe Nations from *Popery* and *Slavery.* You muft all plainly fee, that you are only made ufe of as Inftruments to enflave the Nation, and ruin the Proteftant Religion ; and when that is done, you may judge what you your felves ought to expect, both from the Cafhiering all the Proteftant and *Englifh* Officers and Soldiers in *Ireland,* and by the *Irifh* Soldiers being brought over to be put in your places ; and of which you have feen *fo frefh an Inftance,* that we need not put you in mind of it. You know how many of your Fellow-Officers have been ufed, for their ftanding firm to the Proteftant Religion, and to the Laws of *England* ; and you cannot flatter your felves fo far, as to expect to be better ufed, if thofe who have broke their Word fo often fhould by your means be brought out

There have been many Inftances. in Hiftory of fuborned and fuppofititious Princes, and therefore there was reafon that fufficient Evidence fhould be given in a Cafe of fuch Importance , and which was under fo great Sufpicion. But if there was no reafonable care taken to prevent or remove thefe Sufpicious, then the Parties moft concerned have a right to affert their own Pretenfions in fuch a way as the Law of Nations doth allow.

And in this Cafe no private Depofitions, or confident Affirmations of fuch as are Dependents , or otherwife liable to Sufpicion , can in reafon be taken for fatisfactory Evidence. *p.* 13.

Secondly , There was a further. Juft Occafion for that Expedition, which was the Defign to fubvert our Religion and Civil Liberties. As to the Particulars , they are fully fet down in the Declaration, and need not to be repeated ; That which I am to make out, is, That the then Prince of *Orange* by his Relation to the Crown, had a juft Right to concern himfelf in the Vindication of both , and that this is not repugnant to the Doctrines and Principles of the Church of *England.*

It was not thought difagreeable to them for Queen *Elizabeth* to affift the *Dutch* againft the King of *Spain* ; yet fhe had no fuch reafon for it as our King and Queen had to prevent the fuppreffion of their out of thofe ftraights to which they are at prefent reduced. We hope likewife, that ye will not fuffer your felves to be abufed by a falfe Notion of Honour, but that you will in the firft place confider, what you owe to Almighty God and your Religion, to your Countrey, to your Selves, and to your Pofterity, which you, as Men of Honour, ought to prefer to all private Confiderations and Engagements whatfoever. We do therefore expect that you will confider the Honour that is now fet before you, of being the Inftruments of ferving your Countrey, and fecuring your Religion; and we fhall ever remember the Service you fhall do Us upon this occafion; and will promife you, That we fhall place fuch particular Marks of our Favour on every one of you, as your Behaviour at this time fhall deferve of Us and the Nation; in which we fhall make a great diftinction of thofe that fhall come feafonably to joyn their Arms with Ours; and you fhall find Us to be your well-wifhing and affured Friend,

W. H. P. O.

And another to all the Officers and Seamen in the *Englifh* Fleet.

Gentlemen and Friends,

AS We have given to our Faithful and Well-beloved Admiral *Herbert* a full power, fo we hope that you will give him an intire credit, as to all he fhall fay to you on our part. We have publifhed a Declaration

their own Religion here, and the Rights of that People to whom they were fo nearly related. *p. 15.*

In the beginning of the Reign of King *Charles* the Firft, when I fuppofe it will be granted, That the Doctrines and Principles of the *Church* of *England* were underftood and followed; the King of *Denmark* had taken up Arms, *to fettle the Peace and liberty of* Germany, as he declared : But he met with a great Defeat. Whereupon King *Charles* the Firft thought himfelf concerned to give Affiftance to him : And Archbifhop *Laud* was then employed (as Dr. *Hylin* confeffeth) by the King's Command, to draw up a *Declaration*, to be publifhed in all the Parifhes of *England*; which was read by the King, and approved by the Council, wherein the *Greatnefs of the Danger they were in is fet forth, and the People are exhorted to ferve God and the King, and to labour by their Prayers to divert the Danger.* Wherein lay this Danger? It is there faid to be, *That by the Defeat of the King of* Denmark, *there was little or nothing left to hinder the Houfe of* Auftria *from being Lord and Mafter of* Germany. And what then? Why then *there will be an open way for* Spain *to do what they pleafed in all the Weft Part of Chriftendom.* It feems then, it was not thought difagreeable to the Principles and Doctrines of our Church, to hinder the growth of a Weftern Monarchy, although it be by affifting Subjects claration which contains the Reasons which moved Us to enter upon this Expedition; in which you will see We had no other design than the preservation of the Protestant Religion, and the re-establishment of the Laws and *Liberties* of the Kingdom of *England*, because it is evident that the Papists have resolved the intire ruin of Our Religion in Great *Britain*, as it is effected already in *France:* And to you it is only to be imputed, if they are Masters.

We are persuaded that you already perceive that you are made use of only as an Instrument for the bringing your selves and your Countrey under the yoke of the Papacy, and into Slavery, by the means of the *Irish*, and other Foreigners who are prepared to finish your Destruction And therefore we hope God will inspire you with more salutary thoughts for the facilitating your Deliverance, and for the delivering you from all your Miseries, with your Countrey and Religion.

And this is in all appearance impossible, without your joyning with us, and assisting us, who seek nothing but your Deliverance. And we also assure you, That we will never forget the Services which you shall do us on this occasion; and we promise to give every one particular marks of our favour, who shall deserve it of us and the Nation. We are sincerely your very affectionate Friend,

W. H. P. O.

These

Subjects against their Princes who promote it. *p.* 17.

But yet here is another Difficulty ariseth, concerning the transferring Allegiance from a Lawful Prince, to him that met with unexpected Success in his Design.

And here I shall endeavour to make it plain, That this is not against the *Doctrines and Principles of the Church of* England. *p.* 20.

The *Articles* of our Church declare, *That the chief Government of all Estates of this Realm doth appertain to the Civil Magistrate:* But they nowhere say, That in a Just War the Superior Power cannot be acquired; or that God doth never confer it in an extraordinary method.

The Book of *Homilies* is very severe against *Disobedience* and *wilful Rebellion*; but it is no-where said, That where the Right of Sovereignty is transferred by a Successful War, there is no Allegiance due to those who possess it. *p.* 2.

Ours is only the Case of Just War ; which is allowed by all sorts   *Apage nugas !* of *Casuists*, who do agree, that Allegiance is due to the Party that prevails in it; and if it be due to one, it cannot be due to another, at the same time, although he be living, and do not discharge Persons from their Oaths; for the obligation of Oaths depends on the nature and reason of things, and not upon the Pleasure of those to whom they are made. But where there

Thefe Letters were fpread under-hand over the whole Kingdom, and read by all forts of men; and the reafon of them being undeniable, it had a great force on the Spirits of the Soldiery and Seamen; fo that thofe who did not prefently comply with them, yet refolved they would never ftrike one ftroke in the quarrel, till they had a Parliament to fecure the Religion, Laws and Liberties of *England*; which the Court on the other fide had refolved fhould not be called till the Prince of *Orange*, with his Army, were expelled out of the Nation, and all thofe who had fubmitted to him, were reduced into their power, to be treated as they thought fit.

The particulars of the Prince's March to *London*, where he arrived on the 18th. of *December*; and the very few Skirmifhes that hapned betwixt fome of his and the King's Soldiers, being inconfiderable, fhall not be recounted.

But betwixt his Landing, and coming to Town,

1. The Lord *Delamere* affembled Fifty Horfemen, and at the head of them marched to *Manchefter*; and the next day, to *Boden-Downs*, being then a Hundred and fifty ftrong, declaring his defign to join with the Prince of *Orange*; which he did.

2. On the 22d day of *November*, the Nobility, Gentry, and Commonalty at *Nottingham*, made this Declaration.

there is a Right to govern, there muft be a Duty of Allegiance: And that *Succefs in a Juft War* doth give *fuch a Right*, I could *What Right do you mean?* produce fo many Teftimonies, of all kinds of Writers, as would make the reading of them as tedious, as of thofe in the Hiftory of *Paffive Obedience*. Nay, fome go fo far, as to affert a Right of Sovereignty to be acquired by fuccefs, even in an *Unjuft War*: But we need none of thefe Teftimonies. *So 'tis, as much as by a Juft War.*

But doth not all this refolve this whole Controverfie into a Right of Conqueft, which is not fo much as pretended in our prefent Cafe? *'Tis not a pin-matter whether it does or no.*

* I anfwer, That we muft diftinguifh between a *Right to the Government*, and the *Manner of Affuming it*. The *Right* was founded on the *Juft Caufes* of the War, and the Succefs in it: But the affuming of it was not by any ways of force or violence, but by a Free *Confent* of the *People*, who by a *voluntary Recognition*, and Their Majefties acceptance of the Government, as it is fetled by our Laws, take away any pretence * to a Conqueft over the People, or a Government by Force. *It's a fine thing to be a Schollar.* *But not to an Ecclefiaftical Whimfie of an imaginary Right by the Choice of God.*

WE the Nobility, Gentry, and Commonalty of thefe *Northern* Counties, affembled at *Nottingham*, for the defence of the Laws, Religion and Properties, according to the free-born Liberties and Privileges defcended to Us from our Anceftors, as the undoubted Birthright of the Subjects of this Kingdom of *England*, (not doubting but the Infringers and Invaders of our Rights, will reprefent us to the reft of the Nation, in the moft malicious drefs they can put upon us) do here unanimoufly think it our duty to declare to the reft of our Proteftant Fellow-Subjects, the grounds of our prefent Undertaking.

We are by innumerable Grievances made fenfible, That the very Fundamentals of our Religion, Liberties, and Properties, are about to be rooted out by our late *Jefuitical Privy-Council*, as has been of late too apparent: Firft, By the King's difpenfing with all the Eftablifhed Laws, at his pleafure. 2. By difplacing all Officers out of all Offices of Truft and Advantage, and placing others in their room, that are known Papifts, defervedly made incapable by the Eftaftlifhed Laws of this Land. 3. By deftroying the Charters of moft Corporations in the land. 4. By difcouraging all perfons that are not Papifts, and preferring fuch as turn to Popery. 5. By difplacing all honeft and confcientious Judges, unlefs they would, contrary to their Confciences, declare that

The Cafe of the Allegiance due to Sovereign Powers, &c.

THAT which has perplexed this Controverfie, is the intermixing the Difpute of *Right*, with the Duty of *Obedience*, or making the *Legal Right* of Princes to their Thrones the only Reafon and Foundation of *the Allegiance* of Subjects: That *Allegiance* is due only to *Right*, not to *Government*, though it can be paid only to Government.

It feems to me to be unfit to difpute the Right of Princes; a thing which no Government can permit to be a Queftion among their Subjects. *p. 1.*

And therefore I fhall not meddle with this Difpute, as being both above me, and * nothing to my prefent purpofe.   * *Then you'll fay nothing to the purpofe.*

Subjects have a plain Rule of Duty without underftanding Laws and Politicks, the Intrigues of Government, the Revolutions of States, the Difputes of Princes; which I am fure is both for the fecurity of Governments and Subjects.

If then Allegiance be due, not for the fake of Legal Right, but Government.

If Allegiance be due, not to bare Legal Right, but * to the Authority of God.   * *That is, to Clergy-mens Crochets.*

If God, when he fees fit, and can better ferve the ends of his Providence by it, fets up Kings without any regard to Legal Right or Humane Laws. *p. 2.*   If that to be Law, which was merely Arbitrary. 6. By branding all Men with the name of Rebels, that but offered to juftify the Laws in a legal courfe againft the Arbitrary Proceedings of the King, or any of his corrupt Minifters. 7. By burthening the Nation with an Army, to maintain the Violation of the Rights of the Subjects; and by difcountenancing the Eftablifhed Religion. 8. By forbidding the Subjects the benefit of Petitioning, and conftruing them Libellers; fo rendring the Laws a Nofe of Wax, to ferve their Arbitrary Ends. And many more fuch like, too long here to enumerate.

We being thus made fadly fenfible of the Arbitrary Tyrannical Government, that is by the influence of *Jefuitical* Councils coming upon us, do unanimoufly declare, That not being willing to deliver our Pofterity over to fuch a condition of *Popery* and *Slavery*, as the aforefaid Oppreffions do inevitably threaten; we will, to the utmoft of our power, oppofe the fame, by joining with the Prince of *Orange*, (whom, we hope, God Almighty hath fent to refcue us from the Oppreffions aforefaid) will ufe our utmoft endeavours for the recovery of our almoft ruin'd Laws, Liberties, and Religion; and herein we hope all good Proteftant Subjects will with their Lives and Fortunes be affiftant to us, and not be bugbear'd with the opprobrious terms of Rebels; by which they would fright us to become perfect Slaves to their Tyrannical Infolences and Ufurpations: For we affure our felves, that

If Kings, thus fet up by God, are invefted with God's Authority, which muft be obey'd, not only for wrath, but alfo for confcience fake.

If thefe Principles be true, it is plain, That Subjects are bound to obey, and to pay and fwear Allegiance (if it be required) to thofe Princes whom God hath placed and fettled in the Throne, whatever Difputes there may be about their legal Right, when they are invefted with God's Authority.

And then it is plain, That our old Allegiance and old Oaths are at an end, when God has fet over us a new King: For when God tranffers Kingdoms, and requires our Obedience and Allegiance to a new King, he neceffarily transfers our Allegiance too.

This Scheme of Government may ftartle fome men at firft, before they have well confidered it. *p.* 2, 3. *From you it will ftartle no man of common fenfe.*

The Church of *England* has been very careful to inftruct Her Children in their Duty to Princes; to obey their Laws, and fubmit to their power, and not to refift, tho very injurioufly oppreffed; and thofe, who renounce thefe Principles, renounce the Doctrine of the Church of *England*: But fhe has withal taught, That all Sovereign Princes receive their Power and Authority from God; and therefore every Prince who is fetled in the Throne, is to be obey'd and reverenced as God's Minifter, and not to be refifted; which

F

that no rational and unbiafs'd Perfon will judge it Rebellion to defend our Laws and Religion, which all our Princes have fworn at their Coronation ; which Oath, how well it hath been obferved of late, we defire a *Free Parliament* may have the confideration of.

We own it Rebellion to refift a King that governs by Law ; but he was always accounted a *Tyrant,* that made his *Will the Law*; and to refift fuch a one, we juftly efteem no Rebellion, but a neceffary Defence: And in this Confideration we doubt not of all honeft Mens affiftance ; and humbly hope for and implore the Great God's Protection, that turneth the hearts of his People as pleafeth him beft ; it having been obferved, that People can never be of one mind without his Infpiration, which hath in all Ages confirmed that Obfervation, *Vox populi eft vox Dei.*

The prefent reftoring the Charters, and reverfing the oppreffing and unjuft Judgment given on *Magdalen-College* Fellows, is plain, are but to ftill the People, like Plumbs to Children, by deceiving them for a while: But if they fhall by this Stratagem be fooled, till this prefent Storm that threatens the Papifts be paft, as foon as they fhall be re-fetled, the former Oppreffions will be put on with greater vigour ; but we hope, *in vain is the Net fpread in the fight of the Birds :* For, firft, The Papifts old Rule is, that *Faith is not to be kept with Hereticks* (as they term Proteftants) tho the Popifh Religion is the greateft Herefie. And, fecondly, Queen

which directs us what to do in all Revolutions of Government, when once they come to a Settlement ; and thofe who refufe to pay and fwear Allegiance to fuch Princes, whom God has placed in the Throne, whatever their Legal Right be, do as much reject the Doctrine of the Church of *England,* as thofe who teach the Refiftance of Princes.

For the proof of which, I appeal to Bifhop *Overal's* Convocation-Book. *p. 4.*

I know not how it was poffible for the Convocation to exprefs their fenfe plainer, That all Ufurped Powers, when throughly fetled, have God's Authority, and muft be obey'd : So that here are the Two great points determined, whereon this whole Controverfie turns.

1. That thofe Princes who have no legal right to their Thrones, may yet have God's Authority.

2. That when they are throughly fetled in their Thrones, they are invefted with God's Authority, and muft be reverenced and obeyed by all who live within their Territories and Dominions, as well Priefts as People: If thefe propofitions be true, it is a plain Refolution of the Cafe ; that if it fhould at any time happen, that the rightful Prince fhould be driven out of his Kingdom, and another Prince placed in his Throne, and fetled in the full Adminiftration of Government, Subjects not only may, but muft for Confcience fake, and out of reverence

Queen *Mary*'s fo ill obferving her Promifes to the *Suffolk* Men that help'd her to her Throne. And above all, thirdly, the Pope's difpenfing with the Breach of Oaths, Treaties or Promifes at his pleafure, when it makes for the Service of Holy Church, as they term it. Thefe, we fay are fuch convincing Reafons to hinder us from giving credit to the aforefaid *Mock-fhews* of Redrefs, that we think our felves bound in Confcience to reft on no fecurity that fhall not be approved by a freely-elected Parliament; To whom, under GOD, we refer our Caufe.

3. The King having marched his Army as far as *Salisbury* to meet the Prince, publifhed a Proclamation of Pardon to all fuch of his Subjects as had taken up Arms, and fided with the Prince, provided they deferted the Enemy within 20 days; and promifing Pardon and protection to fuch Foreigners as would come into his Service; and freedom of paffage to others to return into their refpective Countries. But this Proclamation was not at all regarded.

4 When the King was at *Salisbury*, the Popifh Party feeing their Affairs grow every day more defperate, began to employ all their Politicks to invent fome Remedy for them, and then firft formed the Defign of the King's with-drawing, which they grounded upon this Suppofition and Expectation, That within two years, or lefs, the Nation would be in fuch Confufion, that he might return, and have his Ends of it.

5. In

verence to the Authority of God, with which fuch a Prince is invefted, pay all the Duty and Allegiance of Subjects to him.

As for the firft, the Cafe is plain, That the Convocation fpeaks of illegal and ufurped Powers, and yet affirms that the Authority exercifed by them, is God's Authority, and therefore thofe Princes, who have no legal right, may have God's Authority. *p. 5.*

The *Moabites* and *Ara-* *What? not* *mites* never could have *by a Conqueft?* a Legal Right to the Government of *Ifrael*; and yet the Convocation afferts, That when *Ifrael* was in fubjection to them, *they knew, that it was not lawful for them of themfelves, and by their own Authority to take Arms againft the Kings, whofe Subjects they were,* *Prove they* *tho, indeed they were Ty-* *were Tyrants.* *rants.*
The like, they teach of the Kings of *Egypt* and *Babylon. p. 6*

There is no Duty Subjects, as fuch, owe to the moft Legal and Rightful Kings, but the *Convocation* afferts due to all Kings, whom God hath placed in the Throne, by what vifible means foever they obtained it; as to obey and fubmit to them, not to refift them, nor rebel againft them; to pay all Cuftoms and Taxes, to pray for them, nay, to fwear Allegiance to them, if it be required. *p. 7.*

2. The

5. In the mean time the King being unmoveably fixed in a Refolution not to call a Parliament, part of the Army revolted, and went over to the Prince ; and the reſt either difcouraged by the deſertion of them that went, or by the averſeneſs they found in the body of the People from making any oppoſition to the Prince's Arms, or out of a ſenſe that in fighting againſt him, they ſhould fight againſt their own Religion and native Country, appeared ſo lukewarm in the Cauſe, that the King did not think fit to hazard a Battel.

6. Prince *George* of *Denmark* , the Duke of *Grafton*, the Lord *Churchill*, and many others of the Proteſtant Nobility, left the King, and went over to the Prince of *Orange*, then at *Sherborne* ; and on the 25th of *November*, in the night, Princeſs *Ann*, the King's Second Daughter, withdrew privately from *White-hall* with the Lady *Churchill*.

7. The going off of theſe Great Men ſtruck the King with terror, and the Army being before much in diforder , became thereby ſo full of fear and ſuſpicion, that a falſe Alarm being made, whether by deſign or accident, the King and the whole Army left *Salisbury* ; the Army retreating to *Reading*, and the King to *Andover*, and on *Monday* the 26th of *November*, he returned in the Evening to *London*.

8. The firſt thing the King did, being at *London* , was to remove Sir *Edward Hales* from being Lieutenant of the *Tower* , and to put
Sir

2. The *only Enquiry* then is, what the Convocation means by the Government's being *throughly ſettled*. A Prince who is throughly ſetled in his Throne, has God's Authority, and muſt be obeyed ; but when is his Government throughly ſetled ?

No ; it is no part of the Enquiry ; for who cares what either they meant , or you mean ?

Now here it is, That men may impoſe upon themſelves if they will, and if they think it their Intereſt to do ſo ; and may make as little or as much go to a through ſettlement, as they pleaſe ; for the *Convocation* has not determined the bounds of it. *p. 9.*

No ; they left that to D. Sherlock.

The ſubmiſſion of the Prince indeed may be thought neceſſary to transfer a Legal Right ; but the ſubmiſſion of the people, of it ſelf, is ſufficient to ſettle a Government ; and when it is ſetled, then it is the Authority of God , whatever the Human Right be.

All Sovereign Powers , whoſe Power and Government is *throughly ſetled*, muſt be obeyed , whatever their Legal Right be ; for they have the Authority of God. *p. 9.*

All Civil Power and Authority is from God ; for he is the Supreme Lord of the World, and has the ſole Right to govern his Creatures ; and therefore no man can have any Authority but from God: This will be readily acknowledged by all, who believe, that there is a God, and that

Sir *Bevill Skelton*, a Proteſtant, in his room. Sir *Edward* had diſpleaſed the whole City to the utmoſt, by planting ſeveral Mortar-pieces on the Walls towards the City; which tho deſigned only to awe it, had more enraged than afrighted them. So that his Majeſty thought he was not ſafe at *White-hall*, ſo long as Sir *Edward* was Maſter of the *Tower*.

9. On the 28th His Majeſty ordered in Privy Council the Lord Chancellor to iſſue Writs for the ſitting of a Parliament at *VVeſtminſter* the 15th of *January* following. But it was now too late, and the Nation in ſuch a ferment, that it was not regarded what the Court ſaid or did.

10. *Scotland* was by this time almoſt in as bad a Condition as *England*; and ſome of the Nobility and Gentry were ſent up with a Petition for a Free Parliament. The Popiſh Chappels at *Briſtol*, *York*, *Gloceſter*, *Worceſter*, *Shrewsbury*, *Stafford*, *Wolverhampton*, *Bromingham*, *Cambridge* and St. *Edmundsbury*, were about this time demoliſhed, and where-ever the Lords in Arms came, the Papiſts were diſarmed. And in *Norfolk* the Duke of *Norfolk*, their Lord Lieutenant, had a great appearance of the Gentry with him, where he and they declared for a Free Parliament, and the Protection of the Proteſtant Religion. This Meeting was at *Norwich* the firſt of *December*, and after that the ſame Declaration was renewed at *Yarmouth*, and *Lyn*, and the *Suffolk*-Men approved of it, but wanted a Lord Lieutenant to aſſemble and head them

that he made and governs the World.

That Civil Power and Authority is no otherwiſe from God, than as he gives this Power and Authority to ſome particular perſon or perſons, to govern others: For Authority belongs to a perſon, and that Power and Authority which any perſon exerciſes, is not from God, which God never gave him: If he governs without receiving his *Perſonal Authority* from God, he governs without God's Authority. *p. 10.*

But how does God give it him? Perhaps, as he gave you the Holy Ghoſt.

There are but three ways whereby God gives this Power and Authority to any perſons: Either by Nature, or by an expreſs Nomination, or by the diſpoſals of Providence, *p. 11.*

O Sapientia!

Providence is God's Government of the world by an inviſible influence and power, whereby he directs, determines, over-rules all Events to the accompliſhment of his own Will and Counſels. *p. 12.*

Nor does it make any difference in this caſe, to diſtinguiſh between what God permits, and what he does; for this diſtinction does not relate to the Events of things, but to the wickedneſs of men. *p. 12.*

When it comes to action, he over-rules their wicked deſigns, to accompliſh his own Counſels and Decrees; and either diſappoints what they intended, or gives ſucceſs to them, when he can ſerve the ends them in order to the shewing their concurrence with safety.

11. *Bristol* was seized by the Earl of *Shrewsbury* and Sir *John Guise*; the Lord *Lovelace*, who had been seized as he was going to join the Prince, was by the Gentry of *Glocester-shire* delivered out of the Castle of *Glocester*, where till then he had been imprisoned. The Lords *Molineux* and *Ashton* in the mean time seized *Chester* for the King, being *Roman Catholicks*, and *Berwick* stood firm to him; but *Newcastle* received the Lord *Lumly*, and declared for a Free Parliament, and the Protestant Religion. *York* was in the hands of the Associated Lords: and the Garison of *Hull* seized the Lord *Langdale* their Governour, a Papist, and the Lord *Mountgomery*, and disarmed some Popish Forces newly sent thither; and then declared for a Free Parliament, and the Protestant Religion. And *Plimouth* had long before submitted to the Prince of *Orange*.

12. The Popish Party was grown so contemptible, that on *Thursday* the 6th of *December*, there was a Hue and Cry after Father *Peters*, publickly cried and sold in the Streets of *London*. And about the same time came out a Third Declaration in the Prince's name, but not emitted by him; which very much alarm'd the Popish Party, and as it is thought, contributed very much to the fixing and hastning the King's Resolution of leaving the Nation: It was read in many Towns throughout *England* at the Market-crofs, the People

ends of his Providence by their wickednefs; and herein consists the unfearchable Wisdom of Providence, that God brings about his own Counfels, by the free Ministries of men: He permits men to do wickedly, but all Events which are for the good or evil of private men, or publick Societies, are ordered by him, as the Prophet declares, *Amos 3. 6. Shall there be evil in a city, and the Lord hath not done it ?* *p.* 12.

If the advancement to the Throne invetts fuch a Prince with God's Authority, then God gives him the Throne, and does not merely permit him to take it; for no man can take God's Authority, but it muft be given. *p.* 13.

By what means foever any Prince ascends the Throne, he is placed there by God, and receives his Authority from him. *p.* 13.

Sometimes he fuffers an afpiring Prince to invade and conquer a Countrey; but he never fuffers him to afcend the Throne, but when he fees fit to make him King. *p.* 13, 14.

All Kings are equally rightful with refpect to God; for thofe are   *So are all Clergy-men.* all rightful Kings, who are placed in the Throne by God, and it is impoffible there fhould be a wrong King, unlefs a man could make himfelf King, whether God will or no. *p.* 14.

The diftinction then between a King *de jure*, and a King *de facto*, re-   *The Doctor knows not when that Diftinction was born, and when it died.*

lates

People univerſally believing, till ſome time after the Princes coming to Town, that it was really publiſh'd by his Order, and no Counterfeit.

13. On *Sunday* the 9th of *December*, Count *Dada*, the Pope's Nuncio, and many others, departed from *White-hall*, and the next morning the Queen, the Child, and (as was ſaid) Father *Peters*, croſſed the Water to *Lambeth* in three Coaches, and with a ſtrong Guard went to *Greenwich*, and ſo to *Graves-end*, where they embarked for *France*. It's ſuppoſed ſhe carried the Seal from *White-hall*, and caus'd it to be thrown into the *Thames*; for on the 3d of *May* afterwards it was found in the bottom of the River by a Fiſher-man in a Red-bag, between *Lambeth* and *Faux-hall*, and preſented to the King.

Before this, the Marquiſs of *Hallifax*, the Earl of *Nottingham*, and the Lord *Godolphin*, had been ſent by the King and Council to treat with the Prince of *Orange*, and to adjuſt the Preliminaries in order to the holding of a Parliament, who the Eighth of *December* ſent theſe Propoſals to him.

SIR,

THE King commanded us to acquaint you, That he obſerveth all the differences and cauſes of Complaint alledged by your Highneſs, ſeem to be referred to a *Free Parliament*.

His Majeſty, as he hath already declared, was reſolved before this

to

lates only to Human Laws, which bind Subjects, but are not the neceſſary Rules and Meaſures of the Divine Providence. In Hereditary Kingdoms, he is a righful King, who has by Succeſſion a legal Right to the Crown; and he who has poſſeſſion of the Crown, without a legal Right, is a King *de facto*; that is, is a King, but not by Law: Now Subjects are ſo tied up by the Conſtitutions of the Kingdom, that they muſt not pull down or ſet up Kings contrary to the Laws of the Land; but God is not bound by Humane Laws, but can make whom he *Qui bene diſtinguit, bene docet.* pleaſe King, without regard to legal Rights; and when he does ſo, they are true, though not legal Kings, if thoſe are true Kings who have God's Authority. *I challenge the Doctor to quote any good Authority for the Notion of a True King. A True and a Falſe Prophet we know; but a True King is a Novelty.*

We can have but one King at a time; two rival and oppoſite Princes cannot at the ſame time poſſeſs the ſame Throne, nor can Subjects be bound to two oppoſite and contrary Allegiances; for *no man can ſerve two maſters*; and yet Allegiance is due to a King by the Laws of God, and to every King whoſe Subjects we are, that if we could have two Kings, we muſt have two Allegiances.

He is our King who is ſettled in the Throne in the actual Adminiſtration of Sovereign Power; for

King

to call one, but thought that in the prefent ftate of Affairs, it was advifeable to defer it till things were more compofed ; yet feeing that his People ftill continue to defire it, he hath put forth his Proclamation in order to it, and hath iffued forth his Writs for the Calling of it.

And to prevent any caufe of Interruption in it, he will confent to every thing that can be reafonably required for the fecurity of all thofe that come to it.

His Majefty hath therefore fent us to attend your Highnefs, for the adjufting of all Matters that fhall be agreed to be neceffary to the Freedom of Elections, and the Security of Sitting, and is ready to enter immediately into a Treaty in order to it.

His Majefty propofeth, That in the mean time the refpective Armies may be retained within fuch Limits, and at fuch diftance from *London*, as may prevent the Apprehenfions that the Parliament may be in any kind difturbed, being defirous that the Meeting may be no longer delay'd, than it muft be by the ufual and neceffary Forms.

Hungerford,
the 8th of
December,
1688.

Hallifax,
Nottingham,
Godolphin.

King is the Name of Power and Authority, not of mere Right. He,   *Unde derivatur King ?* who has a legal Right to the Crown, but has it not, ought by the Laws of the Land to be King, but is not : But he who is actually fetled in the Adminiftration of the Regal Power, is King, and has God's Authority, tho he have not a legal Right.

Allegiance is due only to the King; for Allegiance fignifies all that Duty, which Subjects owe to their King, and therefore can be due to none but the King.

If then he who has the Legal Right, may not be our King, and he who has not, may ; when any fuch cafe happens, we muft pay our Allegiance to him who is King, tho without a Legal Right ; not to him who is not our King, tho it is his Right to be fo : And the reafon is very plain, becaufe Allegiance is due only to God's Authority, not to a bare Legal Title without God's Authority ; and therefore muft be paid to him who is invefted with God's Authority, who is his Minifter and Lieutenant ; that is, to the Actual King, who is fetled in the Throne, and has the Adminiftration of Government in his hands.

Object. But if this be fo, what does a Legal Right fignifie, if it do not command the Allegiance of Subjects ?

Anfw. I anfwer : It bars all other Human Claims : No other Prince can

To

To this his Royal Highnefs the Prince of *Orange* return'd this Anfwer.

WE, with the Advice of the Lords and Gentlemen affembled with Us, have in Anfwer made thefe following Propofals.

I. That all Papifts, and fuch Perfons as are not qualified by Law, be Difarmed, Disbanded, and removed from all Employments Civil and Military.

II. That all Proclamations that reflect upon Us, or any that have come to Us, or declared for Us, be re-called ; and that if any Perfons, for having affifted Us, have been Committed, that they be forthwith fet at Liberty.

III. That for the Security and Safety of the City of *London*, the Cuftody and Government of the *Tower* be immediately put into the Hands of the faid City.

IV. That if His Majefty fhould think fit to be in *London*, during the Sitting of the Parliament, that We may be there alfo, with an equal number of our Guards ; and if His Majefty fhall be pleafed to be in any place from *London*, whatever diftance he thinks fit, that We may be the fame diftance, and that the refpective Armies be from *London* forty Miles, and that no further Forces be brought into the Kingdom.

V. And

can challenge the Throne of Right ; and Subjects are bound to maintain the Rights of fuch a Prince, as far as they can ; that is, againft all Mankind ; but not againft God's difpofal of Crowns. *p.* 15.

We fwear to maintain and defend his Right, and the Right of his Heirs ; but yet we do not fwear to keep them in the Throne, which may be impoffible for us to do a-gainft a profperous Rebellion. *p.* 16.

Thefe feem to me, to be very plain *Propofitions*, and to carry their own Evidence with them ; and if this be true, it is a very plain Direction to Subjects in all the Revolutions of Government.

The moft that can be expected from them, according to the ftricteft Principles of Loyalty and Obedience, is to have no hand in fuch Revolutions, or to oppofe them as far as they can, and not to be hafty and forward in their Compliances ; but when fuch a Revolution is made, and they cannot help it ; they muft reverence and obey their New Prince, as invefted with God's Authority: *p.* 16.

There are different degrees of Settlement, and muft neceffarily be in fuch new Governments, which feem to me to. require different degrees of Submiffion, or at leaft to juftify them, till it increafes to fuch a full, and plenary, and fetled Poffeffion, as requires our Allegiance, as being notorioufly evident

V. And that for the Security of the City of *London,* and their Trade, *Tilbury.* Fort be put into the Hands of the City.

VI. That a sufficient part of the Publick Revenue be assigned Us, for the Support and Maintenance of our Troops, until the Sitting of a Free Parliament.

VII. That to prevent the landing of the *French,* or other Foreign Troops, *Portsmouth* may be put into such Hands, as by His Majesty and Us shall be agreed on.

Littlecot, De-
cemb. 9. 1688.

This Answer was sent to His Majesty on *Monday* the 10th of *December* by an Express; which when he received, he gave this Just Character of the Prince's Proposals, That they were fairer than he could, or did expect. So that he had no reason then to be afraid of his Person, but might have continued securely in his Palace, and taken care of the Government, and called such a Parliament, as both himself and the Prince desired; which might quietly and effectually have setled this Nation, and prevented all ill Consequences to his Person or Affairs. Yet he resolved to leave the Nation; and ordered all those Writs for the Sitting of the Parliament, that were not sent out, to be burnt, and a Caveat to be entred against the making use of those

dent and sensible to all that do not wink hard, and will not see it.

If the generality of the Nation submit to such a Prince, and place him on the Throne, and put the whole power of the Kingdom into his hands, though it may be, we cannot yet think the Providence of God has setled him in the Throne, while the dispossessed Prince has also such a formidable Power, as makes the Event very doubtful; yet if we think fit to continue in the Kingdom, under the Government and Power of the New Prince, there are several Duties, which in reason we ought to pay him.

As, To live quietly and peaceably under his Government, and to promise, or swear, or give any other security that we will do so, if it be demanded: It is reasonable we should do so, if we think it reasonable to live under the protection of the Government; this all men do in an Enemy's Quarters, and no man blames them for it.

We must pay Taxes to them; for these are due to the Administration of Government, as Saint *Paul* observes; *For this cause pay ye tribute also, for they are the ministers of God, attending continually on this very thing,* Rom. 13. 6. And if we owe our secure possession of our Estates to the protection of Government, let the Government be what it will, we ought to pay for it.

We

those that were sent down.. And at the same time ordered the Earl of *Feverſham* to disband the Army, and diſmiſs the Soldiers.

15. On *December* the 11th, about Three of the Clock in the Morning, the King went down the River in a ſmall Boat towards *Gravesend.* The Principal Officers of the Army thereupon met about Ten of the Clock at *White-hall*, and ſent an Expreſs to the Prince of *Orange*, to acquaint him with the Departure of the King, and to aſſure him, that they would aſſiſt the Lord Mayor, to keep the City quiet till his Highneſs came, and made the Soldiers to enter into his Service.

16. The ſame day the Lords Spiritual and Temporal about the Town, (the then Biſhop of *Canterbury*, *Ely*, and *Peterborough*, being of the number) came to *Guild-hall*, and ſending for the Lord Mayor and Aldermen, made the following Declaration.

The Declaration of the Lords Spiritual and Temporal in and about the Cities of London *and* Weſtminſter, *Aſſembled at* Guild-Hall *the* 11th *of* December. 1688.

WE doubt not but the World believes, that in this great and dangerous Conjuncture we are heartily and zealouſly concerned for the Proteſtant Religion, the Laws of the Land, and the Liberties and Properties of the Subject. And we did reaſonably hope, that the King having

We muſt give the Title of King to ſuch a Prince, when we live in the Country where he is owned for King ; for beſides that, it is a piece of good manners (which is the leaſt thing we can owe to him, under whoſe Government we live) he is indeed King, while he adminiſters the Regal Power, though we may not think him ſo well ſetled in his Government, as to all intents and purpoſes to own him for our King.

Nay, we muſt pray for him under the Name and Title of King, for we are bound to pray for all who are in Authority ; and that Prince is, who has the whole Government in his hands, and has power to do a great deal of hurt, or a great of good ; and this is ſo far from being a fault, that it is a duty, while we take care to do it in ſuch terms, as to not pray againſt the diſ-   ☞
poſſeſſed Prince.

Thus far I think the doubtful poſſeſſion of the Throne obliges us, and it were very happy if no more were required in the beginnings of ſuch a new Government; but when, beſides the poſſeſſion of the Throne, the Power of the diſpoſſeſſed Prince is broken; and no viſible proſpect of his recovering his Throne again ; nay, if it be viſible that he can never recover his Throne again, but by making a new Conqueſt of the Nation by Foreigners, who will be our Maſters, if they conquer, having iffued out his Proclamation and Writs for a Free Parliament, we might have refted fecure under the expectation of that Meeting: But His Majefty having withdrawn himfelf, and, as we apprehend, in order to his departure out of this Kingdom, by the pernicious Counfels of perfons ill affected to our Nation and Religion, we cannot, without being wanting to our Duty, be filent under thofe Calamities, wherein the Popifh Counfels which fo long prevailed , have miferably involved thefe Realms. We do therefore unanimoufly refolve to apply our felves to his Highnefs the Prince of *Orange*, who with fo great Kindnefs to thefe Kingdoms, fo vaft Expence, and fo much Hazard, hath undertaken, by endeavouring to procure a Free Parliament, to refcue us (with as little effufion of Chriftian Blood as poffible) from the imminent Dangers of *Popery* and *Slavery*,

And we do hereby declare, That we will with our utmoft Endeavours affift his Highnefs, in the obtaining fuch a Parliament with all fpeed, wherein our Laws, our Liberties and Properties may be fecured, the Church of *England* in particular, with a due Liberty to Proteftant Diffenters, and in general, the Proteftant Religion and Intereft, over the whole World, may be fupported and encouraged, to the Glory of GOD, the Happinefs of the Eftablifhed Government in thefe Kingdoms , and the Advantage of all Princes and

and no very gentle ones neither ; we may then look upon the new Prince as advanced and fetled by God in his Throne, and therefore fuch a King, as we owe an entire Obedience and Allegiance to.

For we muft not take the confideration of Right into the fettlement of Government ; for a Prince may be fetled in his Throne without Legal Right ; and when he is fo, God has made him our King, and requires our Obedience. *p.* 17, 18. *No, have a care of that.*

The Scripture has given us no Directions in this Cafe, but to fubmit, and pay all the Obedience of Subjects to the prefent Powers. It makes no diftinction, that ever I could find , between Rightful Kings and Ufurpers , between Kings whom we muft, and whom we muft not obey ; but the general Rule is, *Let every Soul be fubject to the higher Powers, for all power is of God.* p. 18.

To fay the *Apoftle* here fpeaks of Lawful Power, is *gratis dictum*, for there is no Evidence of it : The Criticifm between ἐξουσία and δύναμις will not do ; for they both fignify the fame thing in Scripture, either Force and Power, or Authority. *p.* 19.

When the *Apoftle* fays, *All power is of God*, there is no reafon to confine this *to the Legal Powers*, unlefs it were evidently the Doctrine of Scri-

and States in *Chriſtendom*, that may be herein concerned.

In the mean time we will endeavour to preſerve, as much as in us lies, the Peace and Security of theſe great and populous Cities of *London* and *Weſtminſter*, and the parts adjacent, by taking care to diſarm all Papiſts, and ſecure all Jeſuits and *Romiſh* Prieſts, who are in or about the ſame.

And if there be any thing more to be performed by Us, for promoting his Highneſs's Generous Intentions for the publick good, we ſhall be ready to do it, as occaſion requires.

Signed ————

W. Cant.	*P. Wincheſter.*
T. Ebor.	*W. Aſaph.*
Pembrook.	*F. Ely.*
Dorſet.	*Tho. Roffen.*
Mulgrave.	*Tho. Petriburg.*
Thanet.	*P. Wharton.*
Carliſle.	*North and Grey.*
Craven.	*Chandois.*
Ailesbury.	*Montague.*
Burlington.	*T. Jermyn.*
Suſſex.	*Vaughan Carbery.*
Berkeley.	*Culpeper.*
Rocheſter.	*Crewe.*
Newport.	*Oſulſton.*
Weymouth.	

Whereas his Majeſty hath privately this Morning withdrawn himſelf, We the Lords Spiritual and Temporal, whoſe Names are hereunto Subſcribed, being aſſembled in *Guild-hall,*

Scripture, that *uſurped Powers are not of God,* which is ſo far from being true, that the contrary is evident ; *that the moſt high ruleth in the kingdom of men, and giveth it to whomſoever he will,* 4 Dan. 17. which is ſpoke with reference to the *four Monarchies,* which were all as manifeſt Uſurpations as ever were in the World, and yet ſet up by the Decree and Counſel of God, and foretold by a prophetick Spirit : and whoever will confine the Power and Authority of God, *in changing Times and* *Wiſdom will* *Seaſons, in removing* *die with this* *Kings, and ſetting up* *man !* *Kings,* to Humane Laws, ought not to be diſputed with. *p.* 20.

This I'm ſure, The only direction of Scripture is to ſubmit to thoſe who are in Authority, who are in the actual adminiſtration of Government, to reverence and obey them, to pray for them, to pay Tribute to them, *as God's Miniſters, attending continually upon this very thing,* and not to reſiſt them ; but there is not the leaſt notice given us of any kind of Duty owing, or to be paid, to a Prince out of Authority, and removed from the Adminiſtration of Government, whatever his Right may be. *p.* 21.

The Prophecy of the *Four Monarchies* is not yet at an end ; for under the *fourth* Monarchy the Kingdom of *Chriſt* was to be ſet up, and *Antichriſt* was to appear, and the increaſe and deſtruction of *ball* in *London*, having agreed upon, and Signed a Declaration of the Lords Spiritual and Temporal, in and about the Cities of *London* and *Westminster*, assembled at *Guild-hall* the 11th of *December*, 1688. do desire the Right Honourable the Earl of *Pembrook*, the Right Honourable the Lord Viscout *Weymouth*, the Right Reverend Father in God the Lord Bishop of *Ely*, and the Right Honourable the Lord *Culpeper*, forthwith to attend his Highness the Prince of *Orange* with the said Declaration, and at the same time to acquaint his Highness with what we have further done at this Meeting. Dated at *Guild-hall* the 11th of *December*, 1688.

The Lords, before they came down to the City, had appointed the Lord Mayor, Court of Aldermen, and the Common-Council, to be assembled, to concert with them the means of preserving the City and Kingdom; and when the Peers had thus led the way, they presently resolved also on the following Address to his Highness the Prince of *Orange* :

May it please Your Highness,

WE taking into consideration your Highness's fervent Zeal for the *Protestant Religion*, manifested to the World in your many hazardous Enterprises, wherein it hath pleased Almighty God to bless you with miraculous Success, do render our deepest thanks to the Divine

of the Kingdom of *Antichrist* is to be accomplished by great Changes and Revolutions in Humane Governments; and when God has declared, that he will change Times and Seasons, remove Kings, and set up Kings, to accomplish his own wise Counsels, it justifies our necessary, and therefore innocent compliances with such Revolutions, as much as if we were expresly commanded to do so, as the *Jews* were by the Prophet *Jeremiah*. This a man may say without Enthusiasm, or pretending to understand all the Prophesies of the *Revelations*, and to apply them to their particular events; for without that, we certainly know, that all the great Revolutions of the World are intended by God to serve those great Ends; and when God will overturn Kingdoms and Empires, remove, and set up Kings, as he sees will best serve the accomplishment of his own Counsels and Decrees, it is very hard, if Subjects must not quietly submit to such Revolutions: we must not, contrary to our sworn Duty and Allegiance, promote such Revolutions, upon a pretence of fulfilling Prophesies; but when they are made and settled, we ought to submit to them.

No, tho we be upon the point of losing our Laws and Liberties.

We have no direction in Scripture at all about making or unmaking Kings, or restoring a dispossessed Prince to his Throne again; and all the Commands we have in Scripture about Obedience and Subjection vine Majesty for the same, and beg leave to present our most humble Thanks to your Highness, particularly for your appearing in Arms in this Kingdom, to carry on and perfect your glorious Designs to rescue *England*, *Scotland*, and *Ireland* from Slavery and Popery, and in a Free Parliament to establish the Religion, and the Laws and Liberties of these Kingdoms upon a sure and lasting Foundation.

We have hitherto look'd for some remedy for those Oppressions and imminent Dangers, which we, together with our Protestant Fellow-Subjects, laboured under, from his Majesties Concessions and Concurrences with your Highness's just and pious purposes expressed in your Gracious Declaration.

But herein finding our selves finally disappointed by his Majesties withdrawing himself, we presume to make your Highness our Refuge; and do in the Name of this Capital City, implore your Highness's Protection, and most humbly beseech your Highness to repair to this City, where your Highness will be received with universal Joy and Satisfaction.

This Address being approved and Signed, four Aldermen and eight Commoners were appointed to attend his Highness with it.

The same day the Lieutenancy of *London* Signed this following Address to the Prince of *Orange* at **Guild-**

jection to Government, manifestly respects the present Ruling Powers, without any distinction between rightful and Usurped Powers; it seems therefore plainly to determin this Question on the side of the present Powers. *p.* 22, 23.

Let God Almighty turn Kingdoms topsie turvie, as he pleases, the Doctor will always fall upon his feet.

If the Choice and Consent of the people makes a Prince, then no man is a Subject, but he who consents to be so; for the Major Vote cannot include my consent, unless I please; that is the effect of Law and Compact, or Force, not of Nature. If Subjects give their Prince Authority, they may take it away again, if they please; there can be no irresistible Authority derived from the people; for if the Authority be wholly derived from them, who shall hinder them from taking it away, when they see fit? Upon these Principles, there can be no Hereditary Monarchy; one Generation can only chuse for themselves, their Posterity having as much Right to chose as they had. *p.* 24.

If a man gives me a pair of Gloves, who shall hinder him from taking them away again, when he sees fit?

I cannot see where to fix the Foundation of Government, but in the Providence of God, who either by the choice of the major or stronger part of the people, or by Conquest, or by Submission, and the long successive continuance of power, or by Human Laws, gives a Prince and his Family possession of the Throne, which is a good Title against all Humane Claims, and requires the Obedience and Submission.

Guild-hall, and fent it by Sir *Robert Clayton*, Knight; Sir *William Ruffel*, Sir *Bafil Firebrace*, Knights; and *Charles Duncomb*, Efquire.

May it pleafe Your Highnefs,

WE can never fufficiently exprefs the deep fenfe we have conceived, and fhall ever retain in our Hearts, that your Highnefs has expofed your Perfon to fo many Dangers by Sea and Land, for the prefervation of the Proteftant Religion, and the Laws and Liberties of this Kingdom, without which unparallel'd Undertaking, we muft probably have fuffered all the Miferies that *Popery* and *Slavery* could have brought upon us.

We have been greatly concerned, that before this time we had not any feafonable opportunity to give your Highnefs and the World a real Teftimony, That it has been our firm Refolution, to venture all that is dear to us, to attain thofe glorious Ends which your Highnefs has propos'd for reftoring and fetting thefe diftracted Nations.

We therefore now unanimoufly prefent to your Highnefs our juft and due acknowledgments for that happy Relief you have brought to us; and that we may not be wanting in this prefent Conjuncture, we have put our felves into fuch a pofture, that (by the bleffing of God) we may be capable to prevent all ill Defigns, and to preferve this City in Peace and Safety, till your Highnefs's happy Arrival.

We

fion of Subjects as long as God is pleafed to continue him and his Family in the Throne; but it is no Title againft God, if he pleafe to advance another Prince. *p.* 24.

To fay that God fets up no Prince, who afcends the Throne without a Humane and Legal Right, is to fay, that fome Kings are removed, and others fet up, but not by God; which is a direct contradiction to Scripture; it is to fay, That the *Four Monarchies* were not fet up by God, becaufe they all began by Violence and Ufurpation: It is to fay, That God, as well as men, is confined by Humane Laws, in making Kings: It is to fay, That the Right of Government is not derived from God, without the confent of the people; for if God can't make a King without the people, or againft their confent declared by their Laws, the Authority muft be derived from the people, not from God; or at leaft if it be God's Authority, yet God can't give it himfelf without the people, nor otherwife than they have directed him by their Laws.

This is all very abfurd.   *So's all the reft of your Book, Sir.*

The Providence of God removes Kings, and fets up Kings, but alters no Legal Right, nor forbids thofe who are difpoffeffed of them, to recover their Right, when they can. While fuch a Prince is in the Throne, it is a declaration of God's Will, that he fhall Reign for

fome

We therefore humbly defire, that your Highnefs will pleafe to repair to this City with what convenient fpeed you can, for the perfecting the Great Work which your Highnefs has fo happily begun, to the general joy and fatisfaction of us all.

17. After his Highnefs had received certain Intelligence that the King was gone back from *Salisbury* to *London,* he came forward by eafie Journeys, and entred *Salisbury* on *Tuefday* the 4th of *December.* On the 5th, the Earl of *Oxford* came thither to him. The fame day the Lord *Herbert* of *Cherbury,* and Sir *Edward Harley,* and moft of the Gentry of *VVorcefterfhire* and *Herefordfhire,* met at *VVorcefter,* and declared for the Prince of *Orange.* *Ludlow* Caftle was alfo taken in for him by the Lord *Herbert* and Sir *VValter Blunt,* and the Popifh Sheriff of *Worcefter* fecured in it by that Peer. The 7th of *December* his Highnefs came on to *Hungerford*; the 8th, the Lords fent by the King, came thither to him, and had the Difpatch already mentioned: after Dinner he went to *Lidcot.* The 14th, The Commiffioners of the Peers, Common-Council, and Lieutenancy of *London,* prefented three Addreffes to the Prince at *Henly.* The 15th his Highnefs entred *Windfor.*

18. The King was ftopt in his paffage by fome who knew him not, but feiz'd him and his Company as fufpected Jefuits, &c. but being at laft

fome time, longer or fhorter, as God pleafes; and that is an obligation to Subjects to fubmit and obey; for Submiffion is owing only to God's Authority; but that one Prince is at prefent placed in the Throne, and the other removed out of it, does not prove, that it is God's Will it fhould always be fo, and therefore does not diveft the difpoffeffed Prince to recover his Legal Right: *A Legal and Succeffive Right is the ordinary way whereby the Providence of God advances Princes to an Hereditary Throne: And this bars all other humane Claims; but yet God may give the Throne to another, if he pleafes; and this does not deftroy the Legal Right of the difpoffeffed Prince, nor hinder him from claiming it, when he finds his opportunity.* p. 26.

It is a great Queftion, which I am not Lawyer enough to decide; Whether a Commiffion granted by a King out of Poffeffion, be a Legal Commiffion? *p.* 31.

Why, 'tis a Legal Commiffion, but it has not the Authority of God.

Oaths oblige every particular man to do no injury to the King's Perfon or Crown, not to enter into Plots and Confpiracies againft him; and as for actual defence, chearfully to venture his Life and Fortunes with his Fellow-fubjects to preferve the King. But in cafe the great Body of the Nation abfolve themfelves from thefe Oaths, and depofe their King, and drive him out of his Kingdom, and fet up another Prince in laſt diſcovered , and the noiſe of his being detained at *Feverſham* coming to the Lords at *London*, the Lords *Feverſham, Aylesbury, Yarmouth* and *Middleton* were ſent to entreat his return to *White-hall* : whither he came on the 16th in the Evening. But in the mean time the Rabble at *London* demoliſhed the Popiſh Chappel and Convent at St. *John's*, the Convent and Chappel of Fryars in *Lincolns-Inn-Fields* , and the Popiſh Chappels in *Limeſtreet* and *Bucklers-Bury*, and the Chappel at *Wild-houſe.*

19. The King being now at *White-hall* , and the Prince at *Windſor* , the King invites the Prince to St. *James's*; but the Lords at *Windſor* did not think it reaſonable, nor ſafe, either for the King's or the Prince's perſon to be together in one place with their ſeveral Guards. Whereupon the Guards at *White-hall* were diſlodged by Count *Solmes* , by the Prince's order , and the Prince's Guards placed in their room. And the King was that ſame night , being the 17th of *December* , deſired by a Meſſage from the Prince to remove to ſome place at a reaſonable diſtance from *London*, and *Ham* was propoſed. But the King choſe to return into *Kent*, which he did the next day : and got away privately from the Guards, and embark'd for *France*. The ſame day that the King withdrew from *White-hall* the ſecond time , the Prince of *Orange* came to St. *James's*, attended by Monſieur *Schomberg* , and a great number

in his room, it is worth conſidering, Whether ſome private men, it may be but a little handful, are ſtill bound by their Oath, to make ſome weak and dangerous attempts, and to fight for their King againſt their Countrey ; certainly this was not the intention of the Oath ; for it is a National, not a private Defence, we ſwear ; and therefore a *general revolt of a Nation, tho it ſhould be wicked and unjuſtifiable, yet it ſeems to excuſe thoſe, who had neither hand nor heart in it, from their ſworn defence of the King's Perſon and Crown, and to make their compliance with the National Government , innocent and neceſſary.* For an Oath to fight for the King, does not oblige us to fight againſt our Countrey, which is as unnatural, as to fight againſt our King. The ſum is this ; God, when he ſees fit, can remove Kings, or ſet up Kings, without any regard to humane Right, as being the Sovereign Lord of the World , who rules in the Kingdoms of Men, and giveth them to whomſoever he will ; but *Subjects*, in ſetting up, or removing Kings, muſt have regard to Legal Right ; and if they pull down a rightful King, and ſet up a King without right , (*unleſs the Conſtitution of the Government in ſome caſes ſhould allow it*) greatly ſin in it, eſpecially when they have ſworn the defence of the Legal Right, and Legal Succeſſion ; but the Duty and Allegiance of Subjects does not immediately reſpect Right, but the actual Adminiſtration of Government, number of Nobility and Gentry, and was entertain'd with a joy and concourse of the People, which appear'd free and unconstrain'd, and all the Bells of the City were rung, and Bonfires in every Street.

Thus the body of the People being uneasie under the Late King's Government, and not thinking it either their Interest, or their Duty, to support him in it, who had made use of his Authority only to carry on an Interest inconsistent with the welfare of a Protestant Nation, and that by all the Illegal Methods that his Evil Counsellors could advise, or durst put in execution; and who, to awe the People from giving any check to his Career, had not only Judges at hand, that would wrest the Law to serve his Ends, without any regard to their Oaths, or the trust of their Places; but had raised an Army in times of Peace, directly against Law, and in effect had thereby waged war against his own Subjects: The People, I say, being thus affected, either actually join'd with the Prince, or openly declared for him, or testified by other demonstrations their joy for his arrival, and interposing betwixt them and utter ruine. Whereupon the King was left to shift for himself, and flew for protection to his old Ally, the Enemy of God and Man.

The first thing the Prince did when come to Town, after he had

ment, when there is a setled Government in a Nation; for that is God's Authority, which much be obeyed; no man must swear away this, no more than any other part of his Duty; and no man does swear away this by the Oath of Allegiance, as I have already shown. *p.* 3 1, 3 2.

Object. But have not Pyrates and Robbers as good a Title to my Purse, as an Usurper has to the Crown, which he seizes by as manifest force and violence?

Answ. The Outrages of Thieves and Pyrates are very impertinently alledged in this Cause. They have force and violence, which every man must submit to, when he cannot help it; but Sovereign Power is God's Authority, tho Princes may be advanced to it by no honester means than Thieves take a Purse, or break open my House, and take my Money or Goods. The beginnings of the Four Monarchies were no better, and yet their Power was God's. *p.* 34.

This Doctrine of Obedience and Allegiance to *Gen.*49.14. the present Powers, is founded on the same Principle with the Doctrine of *Non-Resistance* and *Passive-Obedience,* and therefore both must be true, or both false; for it is founded on this Principle, That God makes Kings, and invests them with his Authority; which equally proves, That all Kings, who have received a Sovereign Authority from God, and had received the Congratulations of the City by all the Aldermen, and two Common-Council-men for every Ward, and taken care about the Army, was to defire the Advice of fuch Lords as were in or about the Town, and of fuch Gentlemen as had ferved in any Parliament in the Reign of the Late King *Charles*, what courfe to take for the fettlement of the Nation.

Thefe advifed him to take upon himfelf the Adminiftration of publick Affairs, Civil and Military, and the difpofal of the Publick Revenue, and to iffue out Circular Letters for the calling a Convention to meet and fit at *Weftminfter* on the 22d of *January* next enfuing.

Which was done accordingly, and the Elections went on with the greateft liberty that could poffibly be conceived.

The Two Houfes met the 22d of *January*, and the Upper Houfe chofe the Marquefs of *Halifax* for their Speaker; and the Commons, *Henry Powle*, Efq;. After which a Letter from the Prince of *Orange* was read to them, Exhorting them to unity, and fpeed in their Confultations.

The Houfes ordered the 31ft of *January* to be appointed for a day of Publick Thankfgiving to Almighty God for delivering this Kingdom from Popery and Arbitrary Power by means of his Highnefs the Prince of *Orange.* That Day to be obferved in *London* and *Weftminfter*,

and are in the actual adminiftration of it (which is the only evidence we have, that they have received it from God) muft be obeyed, and muft not be refifted. *Set afide this Principle, That all Sovereign Princes receive their Authority from God, and I grant that Non-Refiftance is Nonfenfe; for there is no other irrefiftible Authority, but that of God. p. 36.*

Thefe Principles anfwer all the ends of Government, both for the fecurity of the Prince and Subjects; and that is a good Argument to believe them true.

A Prince who is in Poffeffion, is fecured in Poffeffion by them, (as far as any Principles can fecure him) againft all Attempts of his Subjects, who muft reverence God's Authority in him; and fubmit to him without Refiftance, tho they are ill ufed.

They will not indeed ferve the Revolutions of Government, to remove one King, and fet up another; and if they would, Princes might be jealous of them; for whatever Service they might do them at one turn, they might do them as great Differvice at another: The Revolutions of Government are not the Subjects Duty, but God's Prerogative; and therefore it is not likely that he has prefcribed any certain Rules or Methods for the overturning and changing Government, which he keeps in his own hands, and which when he fees fit to do

Westminster, and ten miles distance; and the 14th of *February* after throughout the Kingdom.

On the 28th of *January* the Commons passed this Vote ; *viz. Resolved , That King* James *the IId having endeavoured to subvert the Constitution of the Kingdom by breaking the Original Contract between King and People ; and by the Advice of Jesuits, and other wicked persons, having violated the Fundamental Laws , and having withdrawn himself out of this Kingdom, hath abdicated the Government, and that the Throne is thereby become Vacant.*

On the 6th of *February* the Lords assented to the Vote.

It will not be material to give a particular Account of the Debates and Conferences that arose, and were occasioned by this and other Votes of the Commons; I hasten to the Conclusion, which was, That on the 12th of *February* the Two Houses fully agreed all things in dispute betwixt them on this manner ; *viz.*

The Declaration of the Lords Spiritual and Temporal, and Commons Assembled at Westminster.

WHereas the late King *James* the Second , by the Assistance of divers Evil Counsellors, Judges and Ministers employ'd by him, did endeavour to subject and extirpate the Protestant Religion, and the Laws and Liberties of this Kingdom.

By assuming and exercising a power of Dispensing with, and suspending

do it , he never wants ways and means of doing.

But when any Prince is setled in the Throne, by what means soever it be, these Principles put an end to all disputes of Right and Title, and bind his Subjects to him by Duty and Conscience , and a Reverence of God's Authority ; which is the fastest hold he can possibly have of them ; for those whom Religion will *No ; Interest is the fastest hold in these cases.* not bind , nothing but Force can.

And therefore these are the only principles which in such Revolutions can make Government easie both to Prince and People ; and if Government must be preserved in all Revolutions, those are the best Principles which are most for the ease and safety of it.

But on the other hand, such an immoveable and unalterable Allegiance, as is thought due only to a Legal Right and Title, and must be paid to none, but to a Legal and Rightful Prince, serves no ends of Government at all ; but overturns all Government, when such a Prince is dispossessed of his Throne, how long soever he continue dispossessed : And what long *Inter-regnums* may this occasion, to the dissolution of Human Societies ? *p.* 43, 44.

I cannot indeed think (neither do I believe, that any body else does) that for a King to leave his Crown and Government in a fright, is in all cases necessarily to be interpreted such an Abdication as is equivalent

to

ding of Laws, and the Execution of Laws, without consent of Parliament.

By committing and prosecuting divers worthy Prelates, for humbly Petitioning to be excused from concurring to the said Assumed Power.

By issuing and causing to be executed a Commission under the Great Seal, for erecting a Court, call'd *The Court of Commission for Ecclesiastical Affairs*.

By Levying Money for, and to the use of the Crown, by pretence of Prerogative, for other time, and in other manner, than the same was granted by Parliament.

By raising and keeping a standing Army within the Kingdom in time of Peace, without consent of Parliament; and Quartering Soldiers contrary to Law.

By causing several good Subjects, being Protestants, to be disarmed, at the same time when Papists were both Armed and imployed contrary to Law.

By violating the Freedom of Elections of Members to serve in Parliament.

By Prosecutions in the Court of *King's-Bench*, for Matters and Causes cognizable only in Parliament, and by divers other Arbitrary and Illegal Courses.

And whereas of late Years, partial, corrupt, and unqualified Persons have been returned and served on Juries in Trials, and particularly divers Jurors in Trials for High-

to a voluntary Resignation; whereby he renounces all future Right and Claim to it. But if he have reduced himself to such a state, that he is forced for his own preservation to leave his Kingdom and Government; it is plain, that in some sense he leaves his Throne vacant too; that is, there is no body in it, no body in the actual Administration of the Government.

Thus far I think Subjects may be very guiltless, who do not drive the King away, but only suffer him quietly to escape out of his Kingdoms; for this is no *Rebellion*, no *Resistance*, but only *Non-Assistance*, which may be very innocent; for there are some cases wherein Subjects are not bound to assist their Prince; and if ever there were such a Case, this was it.

What then shall Subjects do, when the King is gone, and the Government Dissolved, the people left in the Hands of another Prince, without any Reason, or any Authority, or any formed Power, to oppose him? The Government must be Administred by some-body, unless we can be contented that the Rabble should govern.

But *I shall not meddle with that Interval between the going away of the King, and the Prince's coming to the Throne*; but only consider him as placed in the Throne, and

High-Treafon , which were not Free-holders.

And Exceffive Bail hath been required of Perfons committed in Criminal Cafes, to elude the Benefit of the Laws made for the Liberty of the Subject.

And Exceffive Fines have been impofed.

And Illegal and cruel Punifhments inflicted.

And feveral Grants and Promifes made of Fines and Forfeitures, before any Conviction or Judgment againft the Perfons upon whom the fame were to be levied.

All which are utterly and directly contrary to the known Laws and Statutes , and Freedom of this Realm.

And whereas the late King *James* the Second , having *abdicated* the Government, and the Throne being thereby *vacant.*

His Highnefs the Prince of *Orange* (whom it hath pleafed Almighty God to make the Glorious Inftrument of Delivering this Kingdom from *Popery* and *Arbitrary Power*) did (by the Advice of the Lords Spiritual and Temporal, and divers principal Perfons of the Commons) caufe Letters to be written to the Lords Spiritual and Temporal, being Proteftants , and other Letters to the feveral Counties, Cities, Univerfities, Burroughs, Cinque-Ports for the chufing of fuch Perfons to reprefent them, as were of right to be fent to Parliament, to meet and fit at *Weftminfter* upon the 22d day of

and fetled there. And now we can find no alteration in the Ancient Government of the Nation, but only the exchange of perfons ; and all things concur to make this a very advantageous and acceptable Change, excepting fuch difficulties, as ufually accompany fuch Revolutions. *p.* 49, 50.

Legal Rights muft be determined by a Legal Authority; and there is no Authority can take Cognizance of the Titles and Claims of Princes, and the difpofal of the Crown, but the *Eftates* of the Realm : *They indeed are obliged to take notice of the legal Defcent of the Crown ; and if through miftake, or any other caufe, they fet the Crown upon a wrong Head, they muft anfwer for it ;* but private Subjects, who have no legal Cognizance of the matter, are bound by no Law, that I know of, to difown a King whom the *Eftates* have owned, though they fhould think the Right is in another. *p.* 52, 53.

Hitherto have been difplayed the Principles of fome of our Heavenly Guides , with refpect to our Prefent Settlement.

of *January,* 1688, in order to such an Establishment, as that their Religion, Laws and Liberties, might not again be in danger of being subverted; upon which Letters Elections have been accordingly made.

And thereupon the said Lords Spiritual and Temporal, and Commons, pursuant to their Respective Letters and Elections, being now Assembled in a full and Free *Representative* of this Nation, taking into their most serious consideration the best means for attaining the Ends aforesaid, do in the first place (as their Ancestors in like case have usually done) for the vindicating and asserting their Ancient Rights and Liberties, declare,

That the pretended Power of suspending of Laws, or the Execution of Laws, by Regal Authority, without consent of Parliament, is illegal.

That the pretended Power of Dispensing with Laws, or the execution of Laws by Regal Authority, as it hath been assumed and exercised of late, is illegal.

That the Commission for erecting the late *Court of Commissioners for Ecclesiastical Causes,* and all other Commissions and Courts of the like nature, are illegal and pernicious.

That Levying of Money to, or for the use of the Crown, by pretence of Prerogative, without Grant of Parliament, for longer time, or in other manner, than the same is, or shall be Granted, is illegal.

That

The Conclusion *of the whole matter take in the Words of a Worthy Divine, lately delivered in a* Sermon *before the* House *of Commons, viz.*

WE may safely conclude from the late Deliverance which we have found, and the Success wherewith it has been attended since, 1. That God has signally manifested his favour to this our *Church.* And 2. That the *King* is the Instrument whereby he has conferr'd this Favour on us. And from hence there arises a twofold Duty upon us:

1. That we should have a regard and reverence for the Church.

2. That we should pay Honour and Obedience to the King. And,

1. How great a veneration and esteem do we justly owe to that Church, which first rescued us from the Tyranny of the *Roman* Yoke; recovered the pure Word of God from their usurpation and disguise, and instated us in the true light of the Gospel ! A Church, which for the purity of her Faith, and the Regularity of her Institution, has ever since stood the Envy, and endured the brunt of *Antichrist*; and has so many miraculous deliverances to shew, that God has espoused her Cause.

That it is the Right of the Subjects to Petition the King, and all Commitments and Profecutions for fuch Petitioning are illegal.

That the raifing or keeping a ftanding Army within the Kingdom in time of Peace, unlefs it be by confent of Parliament, is againft Law.

That the Subjects being Proteftants, may have Arms for their Defence fuitable to their condition, and as allowed by Law.

That the Election of Members of Parliament ought to be Free.

That the freedom of Speech, and Debates, or Proceedings in Parliament, ought not to be impeached or queftioned in any Court, or Place out of Parliament.

That Exceffive Bail ought not to be required, nor Exceffive Fines impofed, nor cruel and unufual Punifhments inflicted.

That Jurors ought to be duly Impannell'd and Returned, and Jurors which pafs upon men in Trials for High-Treafon ought to be Freeholders.

That all Grants and Promifes of Fines and Forfeitures of particular perfons before Conviction, are illegal and void.

And that for Redrefs of all Grievances; and for the amending, ftrengthning, and preferving of the Laws, Parliaments ought to be held frequently.

And they do claim, demand, and infift upon all and fingular the Premifes, as their undoubted Rights and

Caufe. We have heard with our Ears, and our Fathers have declar'd unto us, the Wonders which he did for her in their days, *and our own eyes alfo have feen the falvation of God.* How he refcued us from an implacable ravenous Herd of Men, who had nothing but numbers to entitle them to a Catholick Church, and with thofe numbers they defign'd to over-power the Truth; with thofe Wolves they thought to have worry'd this little Flock: Againft us alone they bent all their Rage, and whet their Teeth in the late unhappy Reign; and when their fmall ftock of Arguments was fpent, they prepar'd for another kind of onfet. But *God deliver'd us from all the expectation of the* Romans, and fhew'd, that it was not their Church, but ours, that is founded upon that Rock: And I wifh all they that are ftill projecting to overturn it, would for their own fecurity confider this, *That no weapon ever profper'd yet, that has been lifted up againft it.*

What do you think of Oliver Crumwell?

And now for any of us to queftion *the honefty* of our Mother-Church, which we have feen attefted by fo many unqueftionable Proofs, by all the demonftration that the nature of the thing will bear, muft be fomething more than Ignorance, fomething that I am loath to name. *To forfake this guide of our youth, who never deferted us in any times of difficulty, never confulted*

her

and Liberties; and that no Declarations, Judgments, Doings, or Proceedings, to the prejudice of the people in any of the said Premises, ought in any wise to be drawn hereafter into Consequence or Example.

To which demand of their Rights, they are particularly encouraged by the Declaration of his Highness the Prince of *Orange*, as being the only means for obtaining a full Redress and Remedy therein.

Having therefore an intire Confidence, that his said Highness the Prince of *Orange* will perfect the Deliverance so far advanced by him, and will still preserve them from the violation of their Rights; which they have here asserted, and from all other Attempts upon their Religion, Rights and Liberties;

The said Lords Spiritual and Temporal, and Commons assembled at *Westminster*, **Do Resolve,**

That *WILLIAM* and *MARY*, Prince and Princess of *Orange* be, and be declared King and Queen of *England*, *France*, and *Ireland*, and the Dominions thereunto belonging, to hold the Crown and Royal Dignity of the said Kingdoms and Dominions, to them the said Prince and Princess during their Lives, and the Life of the Survivor of them; and that the sole and full exercise of the Regal Power be only in, and executed by the said Prince of *Orange*, in the Names of the said Prince and Princess

her own *safety when she saw her Sons in danger, but boldly oppos'd every Enemy, and stood in every breach :* for us, I say, to desert her upon any score, is such vile ingratitude, as hardly can be parallel'd, but can never be excus'd. *What iniquity have your fathers found in me,* said God, *that ye should forsake me, and follow after other gods.* A very serious Expostulation! a most pathetical Complaint!

And the same thing may be said in behalf of our native Church. What is there in this our way of Worship that can justly give offence? What is there in the substance that the godliest Man can scruple, or the wisest Man can mend? What Supplication or Prayer can be made, for any Blessings, or any Grant, of which our humane nature stands in need, that is not daily and decently offer'd up to God from this our House of Prayer? What Portion of God's Holy Word is there that is not here duly read, and, I hope, faithfully explain'd unto you? What Christian Doctrine have we conceal'd from you, or when have we taught you *for Doctrine, the Commandments of men?* Where have we defrauded you of that which is the Word of God, or impos'd upon you that which is not?

A Prayer for honest Clergymen would do well to be added.

When ye coin'd new Articles of Faith, and obtruded them upon us Jure Divino.

If

Princefs during their joynt Lives; and after their Deceafes, the faid Crown and Royal Dignity of the faid Kingdoms and Dominions to be to the Heirs of the Body of the faid Princefs; and for default of fuch Iffue, to the Princefs *Anne* of *Denmark*, and the Heirs of her Body; and for default of fuch Iffue, to the Heirs of the Body of the faid Prince of *Orange*.

And the faid Lords Spiritual and Temporal, and Commons, do pray the faid Prince and Princefs of *Orange*, to accept the fame accordingly.

And that the Oaths hereafter mentioned, be taken by all perfons of whom the Oaths of *Allegiance* and *Supremacy* might be required by Law inftead of them; and that the faid Oaths of *Allegiance* and *Supremacy* be abrogated.

I A. B. *do fincerely Promife and Swear, That I will be Faithful, and bear true Allegiance to Their Majefties King* W I L L I A M *and Queen* M A R Y.

So help me God.

I A. B. *Do Swear, That I do from my Heart Abhor, Deteft, and Abjure, as Impious and Heretical, this Damnable Doctrine and Pofition,* That Princes Excommunicated or Deprived by the Pope, or any Authority of the See of *Rome*, may be depofed or murthered by their Subjects, or any other whatfoever. *And I do declare,*

If any of thefe Charges can be made out, then we will willingly bear the blame till there is a Reformation; but if they cannot be prov'd upon us, as I am certain that they can't; if our Church has conftantly difcharg'd the duty of a careful Mother, then well may fhe expect from us the obedience of Sons; or elfe cry out upon our difobedience, *What iniquity have you or your fathers found in me ?*

God knows they can.

In the mean while, I wifh every man would confcientiously confider this, That a needlefs Separation is very far from being an indifferent harmlefs thing; and therefore they whofe Confciences will give them leave to communicate with us at fome times, I know not how they can excufe themfelves for not doing always fo; for certainly Union is fo pofitive a Command of God, and the want of it is of fo pernicious confequence to the Souls of men, that nothing but abfolute neceffity can give us a difpenfation; nothing can juftify us for breaking the Unity of the Church, but when the terms of Communion are utterly unlawful; if any man thinks that our terms are fuch, they have their liberty; and we have ours; and fo I hope there may be Charity, although there is not Union amongft us; and therefore leaving every man freely to his own way, as he will anfwer it to God, who cannot be deceiv'd, as well as to his own Confcience, which

I 2   can;

declare, *That no Foreign Prince, Perfon, Prelate, State, or Potentate, hath or ought to have any Jurifdiction, Power, Superiority, Preheminence or Authority Ecclefiaftical or Spiritual within this Realm.*

So help me God.

Jo. Brown, *Cler. Parliamentor.*

The fame day this Declaration bears date, Her Royal Highnefs the Princefs of *Orange* arrived in the River of *Thames* in the Afternoon, and was received with all the Hearty Demonftrations and Expreffions of Joy by the City, that are ufual on fuch occafions.

The 13*th* of *February*, the Lords and Commons ordered the following Proclamation to be publifhed and made.

WHereas it hath pleafed Almighty God in his great Mercy to this Kingdom, to vouchfafe us a miraculous Deliverance from *Popery* and *Arbitrary Power*; and that our Prefervation is due, next under God, to the Refolution and Conduct of his Highnefs the Prince of *Orange*, whom God hath chofen to be the Glorious Inftrument of fuch an ineftimable Happinefs to us and our Pofterity : And being highly fenfible, and fully perfuaded of the great and eminent Virtues of Her Highnefs the Princefs of *Orange*, whofe Zeal for the Proteftant Religion, will no doubt bring a Bleffing along with Her upon

can; let us proceed to the laft thing propos'd, wherein I hope we do all agree; and that is, in paying Homage and Obedience to our Sovereign; and that not only upon a Civil, but alfo upon a Sacred account; not *only for wrath, but for Confcience fake.* Kings are the only Perfons upon Earth unto whom God has given an immediate delegation of his Authority; whom to obey, is to obey his Ordinance; and whom to refift, is to refift his Power : And whofoever denies Obedience to be a religious duty, takes away from the King the faireft Jewel in his Crown, and the ftrongeft Fortrefs in his Dominion.

Civil and Sacred muft be diftinguifh'd.

But this is a Doctrine that has been fo frequently difcufs'd of late; fo learnedly demonftrated, and fo undeniably eftablifh'd amongft us, that there is no need to infift upon it now. Only give me leave to fay, That notwithftanding the unreafonable Cavils of gainfaying men, yet *Paffive Obedience* always was, and I hope always will be, the Doctrine and Practice of the Church of *England.* I am fure *'tis a Doctrine of which no Church need to be afham'd, and no King can be afraid:* And to this I fhall only add, That all that Obedience which the Scripture requires us to pay unto the King, we muft now look upon as devolv'd upon Their prefent Majefties, and properly belonging to Their Claim. *The powers that are* (faith the Apoftle) *are ordained of God*; and upon that account they juftly challenge
our

on this Nation. And whereas the Lords and Commons now affembled at *Weftminfter,* have made a Declaration, and prefented the fame to the faid Prince and Princefs of *Orange,* and therein defired Them to accept the Crown; who have accepted the fame accordingly. We therefore the Lords Spiritual and Temporal, and Commons, together with the Lord Mayor and Citizens of *London,* and others of the Commons of this Realm, do with full confent publifh and proclaim, according to the faid Declaration, *W I L L I A M* and *M A R Y,* Prince and Princefs of *O R A N G E,* to be K I N G and Q U E E N of *England, France,* and *Ireland,* with all

our fubmiffion. And in this point, tho I muft not fay with St. *Paul, that I think I have the Spirit of God;* yet I dare fay, that *I have the Spirit of that Churh in which I was born and bred.* And I dare fay no more : For Crowns and Scepters are very nice, curious things ; fomething a-kin to the Ark of God ; they muft be handled with Ceremony : and tho we approach them with never fo much refpect, yet by an unskilful touch, we may eafily offend ; and 'tis a trefpafs upon Majefty to come too near it.

You mean of a great many of your Church-men : the Spirit of your Church, you underftand not.

the Dominions and Territories thereunto belonging: Who are accordingly fo to be owned, deemed, and taken, by all the people of the aforefaid Realms and Dominions, who are from hence-forward bound to acknowledge, and pay unto them, all Faith and true Allegiance ; Befeeching God, by whom Kings reign, to Blefs King *VVilliam* and Queen *Mary,* with long and happy Years to reign over us.

God fave King *VVilliam* and Queen *Mary.*

John Brown, Clericus Parliamentorum.

The 15th of *February,* the Lords and Commons ordered, That His Majefties moft gracious Anfwer this day, be added to the Engroffed Declaration in Parchment, to be enroll'd in Parliament and Chancery ; which is as followeth.

My Lords and Gentlemen,

THis is certainly the greateft proof of the Truft you have in Us, that can be given, which is the thing that maketh Us value it the more ; and We thankfully accept what you have offered. And as I had no other intention in my coming hither, than to preferve Your Religion, Laws and Liberties : So you may be fure, that I fhall endeavour to fupport them, and fhall be willing to concur in any thing that fhall be for the Good of the Kingdom, and to do all that is in my Power to advance the Welfare and Glory of the Nation. Thus

Thus ended that ftupendious Revolution in *England,* which we have fo lately feen; to the great Joy of the Generality of the Proteftants of *Europe,* and of many of the Catholick Princes and States, who were at laft convinced, that the attempting to force *England,* to return under the Obedience of the See of *Rome* in the prefent conjuncture of Affairs, would certainly end in the Ruin of this potent Kingdom ; and whilft it was doing, the prefent *French* King would poffefs himfelf of the Remainder of the *Spanifh Netherlands,* and the *Palatinate,* and perhaps of the Electorates of *Cologne, Mentz,* and *Triers,* a great part of which he hath actually feized, whilft the Prince of *Orange* was thus glorioufly afferting the *Englifh* Liberty.

The Convention having declared the King and Queen, as aforefaid, proceeded to Declare themfelves a Parliament, to fettle the Coronation-Oath, to Repeal that Claufe in an Oath and Declaration, *That it is unlawful upon any pretence whatfoever, to Take up Arms againft the King, or thofe Commiffioned by him* ; To revive the Adminiftration of the Law, which had been interrupted ; and therein they particularly Enact, That Indictments, &c. for Offences committed betwixt the 11*th.* of *December,* and the 13*th* of *Feb.* 1688, fhould run, *Contra Pacem Regni.*

And by the Firft Act of this prefent Parliament, *The Lords Spiritual and Temporal, and Commons, did Recognize and Acknowledge, That their Majefties were, and of Right ought to be, by the Laws of this Realm, their Soveraign Liege Lord and Lady, King and Queen of* England, &c.

And by the fame Act it was enacted, *That all and fingular the Acts made and Enacted by the laft Parliament, were and are the Laws and Statutes of this Kingdom, and as fuch ought to be reputed, taken, and obeyed by all the people of the fame.*

God fave King WILLIAM *and Queen* MARY.

BOOKS Printed for *Richard Baldwin*.

TRuth brought to light by Time; or the moft re-markable Tranfactions of the firft fourteen Years of King *James*'s Reign. *The fecond Edition, with Additions.*

A New, Plain, Short, and Compleat *French* and *Englifh* Grammer; whereby the Learned may attain in few Months to Speak and Write *French* Correctly, as they do now in the Court of *France*. And wherein all that is Dark, Su-perfluous, and deficient in other *Grammers*, is Plain, Short and Methodically Supplied. Alfo very ufeful to ftrangers, that are defirons to learn the *Englifh* Tongue: For whofe fake is addded a Short, but very Exact *Englifh Grammer*. *The Second Edition.* By Peter Berault.

The *Devout Chriftian's* Preparation for holy Dying. Confifting of Ejaculations, Prayers, Meditations and Hymns, adopted to the feveral States and Conditions of this Life. And on the four laft things, *viz. Death, Judg-ment, Heaven,* and *Hell.*

Victoriæ Anglicanæ; being an Hiftorical Collection of all the Memorable and Stupendious Victories obtain'd by the *Englifh* againft the *French*, both by Sea and Land, fince the *Norman* Conqueft. *viz.* The Battle, 1. Between. K. *Hen-ry II.* and *Robert* of *Normandy*. 2. At *Morleis*. 3. At the Refcue of *Calice*. 4. At *Poicters*. 5. At *Creffey*. 6. At *Agincourt*. 7. At the mouth of the River *Seine*. 8. At *Vernoil*. 9. At *Cravant*. 10. At the Relief of *Orleance*, with the great Actions of the *Lord Salisbury* and *Talbot*. 11. Of *Spurrs*. Dedicated to all the Commiffion'd Officers of the Maritime and Land Forces. *Price ftitcht* 6 d.

Mathe-

Mathematica *Magick*: Or, the Wonders that may be Performed by Mechanical Geometry. In Two Books. Concerning Mechanical Powers, Motions. Being one of the moſt Eaſie, Pleaſant, Uſeful, (and yet moſt neglected) part of Mathematicks. Not before treated of in this Language. By *J. Wilkins*, late Lord Biſhop of *Cheſter*. The Fourth Edition.

The Memoirs of Monſieur *Deagant*: Containing the moſt Secret Tranſactions and Affairs of *France*, from the Death of *Henry IV*. till the beginning of the Miniſtry of the Cardinal *de Richlieu*. To which is added, a particular Relation of the Archbiſhop of *Embrun's* Voyage into *England*, and of his Negotiation for the advancement of the Roman-Catholick Religion here; together with the Duke of *Buckingham's* Letters to the ſaid Archbiſhop about the Progreſs of that Affair: Which happen'd the laſt Years of King *James I.* his Reign. Faithfully tranſlated out of the *French* Original.

A True Relation of the Cruelties and Barbarities of the *French*, upon the *Engliſh* Priſoners of War; being a Journal of their Travels from *Dinant* in *Britany*, to *Thoulon* in *Provence*, and back again. With a Deſcription of the Scituation and Fortifications of all the Eminent Towns upon the Road, and their Diſtance, &c. Faithfully and impartially Performed by *Richard Strutton*, being an Eye-witneſs, and a Fellow-Sufferer.

The State of *Savoy*: In which a full and diſtinct Account is given of the Perſecution of the Proteſtants in the Valleys of *Piedmont*, by means of the *French* Councils: As alſo of the Unreaſonable Conditions and Demands that the *French* King would have put on the Duke of *Savoy*: And of the juſt Cauſes and Motives that induced that Duke to break off from the *French* Intereſt, and join with the *Confederates*: Together with the moſt memorable Occurrences that have ſince hapned there: As alſo the true Copies of all the Letters and Diſpatches that have paſſed between them.

www.ingramcontent.com/pod-product-compliance
Lightning Source LLC
Chambersburg PA
CBHW020254090426
42735CB00010B/1915